MACMILLAN MO

Macmillan Modern Dramatists
Series Editors: Bruce and Adele King

Published titles

Further titles in preparation

MACMILLAN MODERN DRAMATISTS

ALAN AYCKBOURN

Second edition

Michael Billington
Drama Critic, the Guardian

MACMILLAN

First published 1983
Second edition, 1990

Published by
MACMILLAN EDUCATION LTD
Houndmills, Basingstoke, Hampshire RG21 2XS
and London
Companies and representatives
throughout the world

Printed in Hong Kong

British Library Cataloguing in Publication Data
Billington, Michael
   Alan Ayckbourn.—2nd ed—(Macmillan modern
dramatists).
   1. Drama in English. Ayckbourn, Alan, 1939—Critical
studies
   I. Title
   822'.914
   ISBN 0–333–49897–6
   ISBN 0–333–48989–6 Pbk

Contents

Contents

List of Plates

9. *Mr Whatnot* at the Library Theatre, Scarborough, 1976. Photograph © Alec Russell.
10. *Absurd Person Singular*, Scarborough, 1972. Photograph © Ken Boden.
11. *Absurd Person Singular* at the Criterion Theatre, 1973. Photograph © John Haynes.
12. *Just Between Ourselves* at the Queen's Theatre, 1977. Photograph © John Haynes.

Editors' Preface

Modern Dramatists is an international series of introductions to major and significant nineteenth- and twentieth-century dramatists, movements and new forms of drama in Europe, Great Britain, America and new nations such as Nigeria and Trinidad. Besides new studies of great and influential dramatists of the past, the series includes volumes on contemporary authors, recent trends in the theatre and on many dramatists, such as writers of farce, who have created theatre 'classics' while being neglected by literary criticism. The volumes in the series devoted to individual dramatists include a biography, a survey of the plays, and detailed analysis of the most significant plays, along with discussion, where relevant, of the political, social, historical and theatrical context. The authors of the volumes, who are involved with theatre as playwrights, directors, actors, teachers and critics, are concerned with the plays as theatre and discuss such matters as performance, character interpretation and staging, along with themes and contexts.

BRUCE KING
ADELE KING

Acknowledgements

The author wishes to thank Alan Ayckbourn, Heather Stoney, Margaret Ramsay, Peter Cheeseman and Sam Walters for help in tracking down elusive manuscripts; Stephen Wood for his assistance with illustrations; and Ian Watson for permission to quote from his admirable book *Conversations with Ayckbourn* published by Macdonald.

1
In The Beginning

Alan Ayckbourn is popular. He is prolific. And he writes comedies. For all those reasons he is still, I believe, seriously underrated. He is constantly written about as if he were a boulevard lightweight whereas he shows an increasing capacity to handle the darker side of human nature while retaining his technical adventurousness. Studying his plays in detail, one notices the recurrence of certain themes (disillusionment with marriage, horror at masculine insensitivity towards women, dislike of do-gooders and bullish opportunists, sympathy with the feckless and incompetent) within a constantly varying comic format. Emotionally, he has staked out his own particular territory: technically, he is always trying to push the frontiers outwards. So what I shall attempt to do is analyse each play in detail while tracing the links between them and pursuing Ayckbourn's growing maturity of vision.

For London audiences that progress is particularly hard to follow. To the casual, metropolitan eye, it seems as if

1

Ayckbourn sprang fully-armed from the head of some theatrical Zeus in 1967 with a hit comedy, *Relatively Speaking*. It ran for 355 performances at the Duke of York's and ranked as the most mature and accomplished West End debut since Terence Rattigan arrived with *French Without Tears* in 1936. But, of course, the truth is vastly more complicated than that. Not only had a previous Ayckbourn play, *Mr Whatnot*, enjoyed a brief, mildly disastrous run at the off-West End Arts Theatre in 1963; but from 1959 on Ayckbourn had had a number of earlier plays produced both at The Library Theatre, Scarborough and at the Victoria Theatre, Stoke-on-Trent. He had, in fact, paid his dues.

There are six Ayckbourn plays in existence prior to *Relatively Speaking*. None is published; and the scripts now reside in bottom drawers in either Scarborough or Stoke. But digging out these half-forgotten pieces of juvenilia, one finds strong evidence of Ayckbourn's desire to experiment with the possibilities of theatre, of his instinctive technical inventiveness and of his search for the ideal form. None of the early Ayckbourn plays is a masterpiece and I doubt that he would want to see any of them revived; but they do provide fascinating examples of a manifestly talented writer sweating over his craft.

Looking back over Ayckbourn's beginnings, there seems to have been a certain inevitability about his progress towards some kind of artistic career. He was born in Hampstead on 12 April 1939. His father was leader of the London Symphony Orchestra: his mother was a prolific writer of stories for women's magazines and had the foresight to buy the pre-pubescent Ayckbourn his own small typewriter on which he could bang.out his own premature fictions. At the age of seven, the infant Alan was sent off to boarding-school. Even more crucially, his mother embarked on a second marriage to the local bank manager; and Ayckbourn has never denied that his periodic, holiday glimpses of the stormy relationship between his mother and his stepfather lodged firmly in his memory and formed part of his later, rather sceptical vision of marriage.

But there is nothing quite like an English public school to encourage those with artistic inclinations. In my own experience the iron philistinism of such institutions, with their repetitive stress on games, religion and soldiership lightly dusted over with scholarship, acts as a positive incentive to those with dramatic or literary leanings to form their own defensive clique. So it was with Ayckbourn. From the age of 12 to 17, he attended a reputable English public school, Haileybury. He edited the house magazine; wrote the house play at the end of every term; and came into contact with one of those invaluable drama-mad schoolteachers, Edgar Matthews, who organised an annual Shakespeare tour, even taking adolescent Haileybury thespians as far afield as the United States and Canada in a production of *Macbeth*.

Edgar Matthews was a friend of the great, robustly egoistic actor-manager, Donald Wolfit and gave the seventeen-year-old Ayckbourn, whose theatrical instincts were by now stirring, a letter of introduction to him. Thus it was that Ayckbourn, having left Haileybury on a Friday, found himself the following Monday working as an Acting Assistant Stage Manager on a Wolfit revival of Fritz Hochwalder's *The Strong are Lonely*. That was in 1956. From there Ayckbourn went round the repertory circuit in Worthing, Leatherhead, Scarborough and Oxford, graduating from Assistant Stage Manager to Stage Manager and eventually actor.

But the decisive moment of Ayckbourn's young career

came in 1957 when he became a permanent member of Stephen Joseph's Theatre-in-the-Round company at Scarborough. Joseph, the son of actress Hermione Gingold and publisher Michael Joseph, was a lone, dedicated, pioneering enthusiast for the concept of Theatre in the Round which brings the actors and audience into a uniquely close relationship. In 1955 he began mounting twelve-week summer seasons in the round at Scarborough, a bracing, hilly holiday resort on the North Yorkshire coast. Ayckbourn joined him in the third of his Scarborough seasons as both actor and Stage Manager, also going out on arduous winter tours to the Midlands. And it was in the winter of 1958, when Ayckbourn was combining stage management with playing Nicky in John van Druten's *Bell, Book and Candle*, that he wrote his first play. Ayckbourn did not care for his lightweight role and said so. To which Stephen Joseph replied: 'If you want a better part, you'd better write one for yourself. Write a play, I'll do it. If it's any good'. And done it was at Scarborough in the summer of 1959.

It was called *The Square Cat* and, like all of Ayckbourn's first four plays, was written under the name of 'Roland Allen'. Looking at it now what is striking is the fledgling Ayckbourn's ability (he was nineteen when he wrote it) to endow 'a cool comedy in three acts' with some of the insane complexity of farce and with hints of suburban despair. In that sense the play, despite some rough edges, is an interesting harbinger of what is to come. Admittedly the plot itself rests on a somewhat shaky premise: Alice, a repressed, forty-two-year-old wife and mother of two grown-up children, makes a secret rendezvous with a guitar-twanging rock singer at a twenty-room Surrey country house belonging to her absent second cousin. Her innocent ambition is simply to dance with her

4

rock-star pin up; but his motives for coming, since he thinks she is a single woman, are clearly somewhat more dubious.

You have to swallow hard to accept the initial idea (but then you have to do so in *She Stoops To Conquer*). Once that is done, Ayckbourn develops the situation with a good deal of inventive flair. In the first act, after some huffing and puffing from Alice's outraged husband and bovine son, both of whom unexpectedly turn up, the rock idol Jerry Wattis arrives and turns out to look less like a homegrown Presley than a sixth-form classics student with dark suit and thick-rimmed glasses. But just as Alice's husband and son are chuckling over the destruction of her fantasies, the schizoid hero reappears as his loud, guitar-plucking public self.

In the second act, the situation gets more complex. In his shy, quiet private persona (real name, Arthur Brummage) the hero finds himself falling instantly in love with Alice's pretty daughter, Susan, while as his hectic public self he has to satisfy Alice's own suppressed longing for glamour and excitement. In one very funny breakfast scene he has to keep changing clothes and identities depending on which of the women is in the room at the time. The third act consists of a noisy, uproarious party in which Alice gets drunk on gin, her increasingly jealous husband chases the antic Jerry out of the house with a battle-axe and Susan introduces everyone to her polite, soberly-dressed, newly-arrived fiancé. He is – surprise, surprise! – Arthur Brummage whose double identity Alice signally fails to recognise.

What the play shows above all is Ayckbourn's delight in the theatrical possibilities of role-switching. There is nothing psychologically very remarkable in the discovery that inside every pop or rock star there is a quiet homebody struggling to get out (this, after all, is 1959 when idols like Cliff Richard and Adam Faith were keen to stress their everyday niceness). But Ayckbourn knows how to make good use of a schizoid hero roaming around a twenty-room house and forced to play Jekyll and Hyde to two different women: in a part obviously written to show off his own acting abilities, he even has the mild Arthur Brummage mutating into the louche Jerry Wattis in front of the audience. He also orchestrates very well the farcical confusion of the climactic party with the outraged dad taking wild swings at the intrusive pop star with a battle-axe.

But although the play ends with a happy marital reunion, what is significant is the early introduction of one of Ayckbourn's recurrent themes: the wife whose own personality is cramped and frustrated by a totally uncomprehending husband. The assumption is that Sidney, the husband, was once a moony romantic (he even gets to sing a French honeymoon song, 'Je raconte une histoire triste' to the guitar) but that twenty years of marriage have turned him into a stale old sourpuss. 'Every morning,' says Alice, 'I've sat and watched you grunt your way through breakfast.' So Alice seeks vicarious escape through the 'warm, vital, ebullient, forceful personality' of the hip star who ironically turns out to be a square cat underneath. The idea holds up even today when millions of housewives and mums fantasise about Barry Manilow. But, more importantly, within the format of a well-plotted rep comedy, Ayckbourn was securely planting an idea to which he was to return time and time again: that of an unassuageable female discontent.

The Square Cat was a great success when seen at the Scarborough Library Theatre in the summer of 1959. It was quickly followed that winter by another 'Roland

Allen' play, *Love After All*, of which not even Ayckbourn
has a script. This was a reworking of *The Barber of Seville*
in an Edwardian setting with a mean old father trying to
marry his daughter off to a rich heir. It was directed in
December 1959 by Clifford Williams, who a year later also
worked on Ayckbourn's first attempt at a children's show,
Dad's Tale. This began with a synopsis by David
Campton, Scarborough's resident dramatist, based on
Mary Norton's classic novel, *The Borrowers*. The intended
collaboration between Campton and Ayckbourn never
came off so the latter went his own way, writing the piece
both for the Scarborough company and for the British
Dance Drama Theatre (under Gerald Bagley) who did not
get together until quite late in rehearsals.

This combination of narrative and ballet sounds like a
recipe for disaster. But although the show never got an
audience ('we were actually doing it at a time when there
weren't any children around', says Ayckbourn), it does
have a blend of free-flowing imagination and robust
comedy. It is the kind of play that only someone deeply in
love with the theatre could have written. The story is told
by Martin, an interior decorator, and looks back to his
own family's Christmas five years ago: a rags-to-riches
Christmas that begins in abject poverty and that ends with
a feast of plenty because Martin's Dad claims a £250
reward on some stolen silverware which a friend has
dumped on him just as he is about to be nicked.

A simple enough tale. But what is interesting is how,
even at this early stage, Ayckbourn experiments with
different ways of telling it. Long before David Halliwell
began to explore the possibilities of multi-viewpoint
drama, Ayckbourn shows us a single incident from several
points of view. Thus at one moment Martin's hard-up
family find that all their neighbours' Christmas goodies

have inadvertently been delivered to them. According to Martin's Auntie, who butts in to give her version, what then happened was that the jolly neighbours came round, as the turkey was being cooked, to claim their goods in a spirit of festive harmony. Martin then gives us the unsentimental truth which is that the furious neighbours barged in and angrily reclaimed their turkey while Dad and Martin stuffed pork chipolatas and spuds under their jackets.

Ayckbourn also spices the story with plenty of visual gags such as the family furniture being taken out of one door by a removal man and brought back in another door as Dad whips it off the back of a lorry. Without ever descending into the mimsy tweeness of so much children's theatre, *Dad's Tale* also manages to integrate the dance-drama element with the main story. Martin's Auntie puts the family's sudden reversal of fortune down to a group of little people called The Tinies (whom we see busily at work throughout). Dad, however, is sceptical about their existence and rashly says at the end, 'Emily, if you saw little people then I'm a budgerigar'. At which point, the Tinies grab hold of Dad's arms and start flapping them about as he flies off into the night. It may not be great drama; but it does show Ayckbourn's ability to endow a *Christmas Carol*-like tale of poverty-to-plenitude with a sparky freshness.

At this apprentice stage of his career, Ayckbourn was of course doing two things simultaneously: writing to commission for Stephen Joseph and exploring the range of his own talent. We see these two factors coming together in the last of the 'Roland Allen' plays, *Standing Room Only*, which was first performed at the Library Theatre, Scarborough in July 1961. Stephen Joseph was obsessed with the idea of overpopulation and wanted a play set on

In The Beginning

Venus where the Earth's surplus humanity had been despatched. What he actually got was 'A new traffic-jam comedy' set on a marooned bus in Shaftesbury Avenue in 1997. It is certainly an original piece of work; and it is interesting to note that thirteen years later Peter Nichols in *The Freeway* wrote a not dissimilar play about an England swamped by motor cars. Both plays even contain episodes involving the delivery of a traffic-jammed baby. But whereas Nichols's play is a ruthless attack on the ultimate logic of the acquisitive society (the ruling party has achieved power by promising a car for every family), Ayckbourn's is more of a hymn to human adaptability and the survival of the nuclear family against insuperable odds.

Ayckbourn takes as his setting an immobilised, lived-in double-decker in Shaftesbury Avenue. The background is a state-controlled, post-Orwellian, 1997 world in which traffic stretches from London to Birmingham, in which the population require movement passes and in which women have to take an Advanced Maternity and Housewives Exam before being allowed to breed. But in this bleak futuristic nightmare we see a London bus driver, with two grown-up daughters, who has turned his vehicle into a cosy home-from-home with flowering plants under the bonnet and who keeps up a desperate pretence of normality. The tone, in fact, is whimsically jokey with Pa taking his name, Hammersmith, from the bus's destination board.

The dramatic crisis comes when Pa takes on board Paul, a fugitive State Illegitimate Child posing as a bus Inspector. Paul, however, is able to stay because he knows that Pa's daughter, Nita, has become illegally pregnant without taking her Maternity Exam. When she automatically fails that exam (because the government has arbitrarily decided to prohibit further breeding), Paul, Pa

9

and Nita's pompous financé rally round to deliver the outlawed baby with the help of cleaning buckets. The play had many different endings (including several written when a West End theatrical manager, the late Peter Bridge, took out an option on the play for a production that never transpired) but in its original form it concludes with Nita and her financé, having been ejected from a hoped-for room by a gang of muscular clergymen, returning once more to the jovial communal squabbling of the family bus. Even in the authoritarian world of 1997, the nuclear family survives.

The first thing to strike one is how completely the play overturns Stephen Joseph's original prescription. He wanted a play about the hazards of overpopulation: what he actually got was a hymn to the joy of procreation. Indeed Ayckbourn, a twenty-two-year-old father and a reflex libertarian, sketches in pretty deftly a nightmare future world in which the state licenses you to breed, in which people do their furtive courting in Government Multiple Stores and in which the St Paul's Demolition Scheme is proceeding apace. Commissioned to write one play, the individualistic Ayckbourn turned in another. But if I had to categorise the play it would be as a latter-day Ealing comedy: it shows a little pocket of privileged eccentricity surviving in a world strangulated by government interference and bureaucracy. Thus we have an old party in a neighbouring Vice-Consul sawing away on his violin. We have an elderly passenger (the natural Kathleen Harrison or Gladys Henson role) who pops in every day for a cuppa or a chat. And we have Pa, on the first sighting of a new passenger, passing on to his daughter the traditional techniques of annoyance:

PA: . . . Where's all the artistry I taught you? This is a

historical moment. We can't let it pass without mucking him about a bit first.

NITA: How about the all-change technique? Then I'll get on, tell him he's on the wrong bus and as soon as he gets off you be there to tell him he's on the right one.

PA: That's a bit crude. Anyway, the railways perfected that one. I know, we'll give him the terminus delayed-start. Whilst constantly remaining within full sight of the passenger, we approach the bus several times as if intent upon commencing a journey. Then at the last moment, we shoot off in different directions, reassemble and start all over again. How about that?

Obviously old techniques die hard. This lightly optimistic piece reveals Ayckbourn's early penchant for farce with the menfolk trying to feign a breezy normality and keep a snooping visitor at bay while ferrying buckets of water for Nita's delivery, which is to be announced by three rings on the bell for a boy and four for a girl. Clearly the play became rather unwieldy when it was optioned by Peter Bridge and endlessly rewritten for a variety of different stars (including Sid James) and for a spectacular climax in which the helicopter cranes would lift the stationary traffic into the sky. But, in essence, it is a simple, cheerful, friendly play that takes an Absurdist situation of a society that has ground to a halt (later used not only by Peter Nichols but also by Jean-Luc Godard in his film *Weekend*) and shows how even so the urge to carry on the race continues. Instinct wins out over a totalitarian ethos (as it was to do twenty years later in *Way Upstream*); and, as the family are finally reunited in the squalid, frantic, overcrowded bus, one feels Ayckbourn is standing up for his own individual right to do the play he wanted rather than the one that was expected of him.

Alan Ayckbourn

With a succession of promising plays behind him,
Ayckbourn moved in 1962 from being actor–writer with
Stephen Joseph's Library Theatre Company in
Scarborough to the Victoria Theatre, Stoke-on-Trent.
Ayckbourn was in at the beginning working as Associate
Director under Peter Cheeseman, a rotund, bearded
dynamo who in the 1960s was to pioneer a whole new
brand of regional documentary and to make the Victoria
Theatre one of the most famous in the land. But the
beginnings were less auspicious. After reviving *Standing
Room Only* at Stoke, Ayckbourn wrote a new children's
show called *Xmas v Mastermind* which he describes
unequivocally as 'the most disastrous play I've ever done'.
Peter Cheeseman, who directed it at Stoke in the cruel
winter of 1962, confirms that it was not exactly a walloping
hit.

'It was our first attempt', he says, 'at a Christmas play
for children and it happened to coincide with a winter of
record cold. We did not realise then that children's
audiences need most exclusive matinee scheduling and put
it on in the evening to audiences of two or three wrapped in
blankets with thermos flasks, etc. I can distinctly
remember seeing the actors' breath on stage as we had only
rudimentary boilers.'

It was indeed a ferocious winter; but one has also to
concede Ayckbourn's point that it is not a terribly good
play. It consists of a running battle between Father
Christmas and a criminal Mastermind known as The
Crimson Gollywog. That's fine for starters. But the play
gets bogged down in a barrage of plot. A left-wing agitator
is sent in by Mastermind to foment industrial unrest in
Fairyland. Father Christmas's fairy helper is abducted. A
couple of bumbling cops try to intervene and mistake
Father Christmas for Mastermind. There are signs of

Ayckbourn's natural visual inventiveness with Gollywog's gang at one point all cramming into a phone booth; and diaphonous whimsy is kept at bay through Mastermind sitting in his lair listening to a record full of groans and screams and evil laughs called 'Songs For Swinging Sadists'. Obviously it is the work of an agile mind. But children's theatre requires clarity, a straight-driving narrative and an obvious focus of sympathy which this, for all its deft touches, does not have.

If *Xmas v Mastermind* perished in the Stoke mid-winter, Ayckbourn's next play for the theatre, *Mr Whatnot*, proved that he was a young dramatist (now twenty-four) of startling originality, always trying to push the frontiers outwards. The play itself had a chequered history as it enjoyed great success at Stoke-on-Trent in November 1963 and was then critically slaughtered when it came to the Arts Theatre, London in August 1964 directed by Warren Jenkins with a remarkable cast including Ronnie Barker, Judy Campbell, Marie Lohr and Judy Cornwell. As at Stoke, Peter King played the eponymous hero; but the chemistry of the new team did not work and the show was, by all accounts, overproduced, overdecorated, overprettified. Alan Brien in *The Sunday Telegraph* was in fact moved to describe the show as 'a nursery hallucination of Christopher Robin after a debauch of cream buns and a matinee of *Rookery Nook*'.

Yet it was, and is, an audacious piece of work: an attempt to translate the techniques of silent-screen comedy to the theatre. Its inspiration is clearly that of early Chaplin and the Tati of *Monsieur-Hulot's Holiday*. But what is fascinating is that it combines a miming hero with the kind of cartoon dialogue you expect to find in elongated strip-bubbles and a full battery of sound effects. The constant peril of mime in the theatre is that it is abstracted from narrative and becomes a display of pure technique dwindling into what Alexei Sayle calls 'some white-faced dildo in a red nose walking into the wind'. But Ayckbourn avoids mimsy-whimsy by placing his hero in a precise situation and by celebrating straightforward physical lust.

The protagonist, Mint, is in fact a piano tuner invited professionally to a country house called The Grange. The Grange is inhabited by walking caricatures of the Loamshire school of English comedy who are so far-out as to be almost surreal. Thus we have the myopic Lord Slingsby-Craddock and his socialite wife, a huntin', shootin' and fishin' Tweedy Lady, the heroine Amanda who is 'a vacant, beautiful, willow-like debutante with a high, thin voice that is almost back-projected' and Amanda's chinless wonder of a fiancé. Cecil. Listening to their discovery of problems with the piano, you feel Ayckbourn is getting his revenge on the drawing-room dialogue he often had to cope with as an actor in rep:

CECIL: Oh, I say.
LORD C: What the devil's the matter?
CECIL: It's flat. Piano's flat. Flat as a pancake.
AMANDA: Pancake (*she screams with laughter*). Pancake – flat as a pancake (*she goes into hysterics*).
LORD C: Bally thing can't be flat. Bally thing's brand new. Send the bally thing back if the bally thing's flat.
CECIL: Flat. Absolutely flat.
AMANDA: Flat as a pancake (*she laughs*).
LADY C: Amanda. Control, darling.
AMANDA: (*contritely*): Sorry mummy.

So we have a silent hero pitched into this world of Debrett daguerrotypes and bringing with him a touch of

14

rantipole chaos. Mint falls for Amanda: she for him, which leads to a desperate rivalry between Mint and Cecil with the two of them, at one point, trying to play the piano at the same time and swivelling round on the stool alternately bashing out Twelfth Street Rag and Beethoven's Moonlight Sonata. At first brutally rejected by the country-house caricatures, Mint then finds himself treated as a guest by Lord Slingsby-Craddock (an aristocratic Mister Magoo) and sucked into a whole series of weekend rituals. There is a mimed, plip-plop tennis match that ends with Mint running round to his opponent's side of the net and winning the game by putting the ball out. An extraordinary tea party escalates into a wartime military bombardment with cress rolls being hurled to the sound of whistling shells and machine-gun fire and Mint seizing the honours (and the girl) by tossing an imaginary hand-grenade into the enemy camp. A classic dinner-party scene has Mint draining his glass of wine each time the butler goes to refill it, losing his steak on the floor and sliding under the table from whence his hand constantly appears to switch round the other guests' glasses. Mint comes to represent Chaos, Misrule, the Comic Spirit of Anarchy. Even after his abduction of Amanda has been thwarted and the heroine has been married off to the dismal Cecil, Mr Whatnot will not lie down. The play ends with Amanda tucked into her solitary bridal bed and a pair of feet appearing at the foot of the bed, one on either side of hers. As a hand reaches out from under the bedclothes to switch off the light, she lets out an ecstatic little cry of 'Mr Whatnot'.

The play is not only a tribute to tumescent anarchy. It also reminds us that for the most part dramatists make scant use of the varied language of theatre. Ayckbourn is here trying to stretch and flex our imaginations so that we conjure up ferocious, five-foot tall dogs, insistently clicking billiard balls, a chase through the English countryside, a couple of young lovers gingerly picking their way across a ploughed field. Simply because it uses the standard country-house setting, it is foolish to overlook the fact that *Mr Whatnot* is actually a rather bold and adventurous play.

It is also worth noting that 1963, the year of its composition, was a time in which other writers and directors were making assaults on the English naturalist tradition. At the Theatre Royal, Stratford East, Joan Littlewood and her company were helping to concoct that amazing, anti-jingoist blast, *Oh What a Lovely War*, with its stunning counterpoint of sentimental song and neon-lit statistic. At the Chichester Festival Theatre John Arden's *The Workhouse Donkey* was putting a whole North-country community on stage and turning a story of complex civic corruption into a monstrous Bacchic spectacle. At the Mermaid *The Bed-Sitting-Room* by Spike Milligan and John Antrobus was presenting us with a decrepit peer who threatened to mutate into a Paddington bed-sit in a post-nuclear world. And at the Arts James Saunders's *Next Time I'll Sing to You* was debating the very nature of illusion and reality through the figure of an historically authenticated Essex hermit. The early 1960s was a period of vehement theatrical transition; and *Mr Whatnot*, however unsung on its arrival in London, was a part of that ferment.

Ayckbourn himself tends to be publicly rather dismissive about his early work; and, with the exception of *Mr Whatnot*, little of it yearns for revival. Yet his first half-dozen plays provide plenty of evidence of a questing theatrical imagination. Consider. By the age of twenty-five he had explored the possibilities of schizoid double identity

(*The Square Cat*); written a children's play combining narrative and ballet (*Dad's Tale*); created an eccentrically apocalyptic comedy set aboard a stationary double-decker in Shaftesbury Avenue (*Standing Room Only*); done a second Christmas show built around the possibility that Yule, like Giraudoux's Trojan War, might not take place (*Xmas v Mastermind*); and dipped an elegant toe into the icy West End water with a comedy combining mime and speech (*Mr Whatnot*). As Eric Rhode noted in a review of *Mr Whatnot* in *Plays and Players*: 'You cannot accuse Alan Ayckbourn of being mean. He seems to have fallen in love, quite splendidly, with everything theatrical'. Like most people in love he had occasionally fallen flat on his face and tried to do too much at once. But there was little doubt of his adventurous talent. The key question was whether he could now harness it to rich themes and well-structured plots.

2

The Plots Thicken

Ayckbourn had thrown up his job as Associate Director at Stoke-on-Trent in the summer of 1964 partly on the assumption that *Mr Whatnot* would take off in London and partly because he and Peter Cheeseman entertained rather different ideas about theatre. 'Our main argument', Ayckbourn told Ian Watson, 'revolved around the fact that Peter believed essentially (and this is to put it a bit crudely) that no actor could do anything unless he fully understood the concept. That is to say, no actor could play a nuclear scientist unless he had read all the books about nuclear science. I said: "No, that's not true: the most stupid actors can often play brilliant nuclear scientists. If the script is good, they convince you; and it isn't necessary to always break everything down and examine it to that extent, and iron out what is the truth".'

Having parted company with Stoke, Ayckbourn joined the BBC in Leeds as a radio drama producer: a job to which he was recommended by a senior BBC producer, Alfred Bradley, who has been a great father figure to numerous Northern writers. Ayckbourn stayed six years with the BBC and during that time he wrote six plays, beginning with *Meet My Father* which Stephen Joseph commissioned for the Scarborough summer season in 1965. As Ayckbourn himself says in his published introduction to the piece: 'Stephen asked me simply for a play which would make people laugh when their seaside summer holidays were spoiled by the rain and they came into the theatre to get dry before trudging back to their landladies. This seemed to me as worthwhile a reason for writing a play as any so I tried to comply'. From such humble beginnings came a play that, under the title of *Relatively Speaking*, opened at the Duke of York's, London, in March 1967 with a stellar cast comprising Michael Hordern, Celia Johnson, Richard Briers and Jennifer Hilary, with Nigel Patrick directing. It ran for 355 performances and established Ayckbourn as the kind of popular comic writer for whom the West End had long been ravenous. Even Noel Coward, in the privacy of his diaries, gave it his imprimatur: 'I saw an enjoyable play by Alan Ayckbourn called *Relatively Speaking* in which everyone was good and Celia superb'. Which is interesting in that Ayckbourn increasingly (if misleadingly) came to be seen as the natural successor to Coward.

'Relatively Speaking'

What was it that made this seemingly lightweight play so durably popular? With hindsight, one can see that the play anticipates Ayckbourn's later preoccupation with gruesomely uncomprehending husbands and neglected wives, with quietly rotting marriages and adulterous sex. But the basic truth is that the play is a stunning piece of comic craftsmanship which takes a simple misunderstanding – a man who airily mistakes his girlfriend's lover and the lover's wife for her parents – and keeps it unbelievably afloat for a couple of hours. I do not believe the device would work if the characters were not anchored in some kind of reality and if Ayckbourn did not have something to say about the relations between the sexes. But what takes one's breath away is his ability to wring so many variations on a single joke.

Admittedly the joke takes a bit more setting up than is usual in the later plays with their almost Aristotelian regard for dramatic unities. The play is written in four scenes, the first of which takes place in a London bed-sit at seven o'clock on a Sunday morning. Ginny, the tenant, is having a fling with a nice, shy, though sexy, young man called Greg. But our suspicions (and Greg's) are aroused by a number of things: mysterious phone calls, piles of flowers in the bath, drawers full of chocolate boxes and, above all, a tell-tale pair of black slippers under the bed. Ginny invents a series of more and more blatant lies to explain away each of these. She also implausibly suggests that a scrawled address (The Willows, Lower Pendon, Bucks) on the back of a cigarette packet is a reminder of where her parents live. So, when she goes off to visit them for the day, Greg impulsively decides to follow her, partly to satisfy his curiosity and partly to ask for her hand in marriage.

In fact, Ginny is visiting her married ex-lover and former boss, Philip, to put an end to their *affaire*. What complicates matters is that Philip vaguely suspects his own wife, Sheila, is having a bit on the side, and that Greg arrives on the scene before Ginny. So what makes this Sunday morning in Bucks fizz is that Greg assumes that Philip is his future bride's father while Philip mistakes Greg for his wife's lover. When Ginny arrives too, the plot achieves dizzying proportions with Philip and Ginny having to act out a dual role: father-and-daughter in front of Greg, boss-and-secretary in front of Sheila. Eventually Sheila tumbles to what is going on and deftly manages to get her errant husband to foot the bill for a six-week honeymoon trip for Ginny and Greg. So the young lovers depart with the innocent Greg never having realised the elaborate deceptions being played and leaving behind the tell-tale pair of black slippers originally found under Ginny's bed. As the curtain falls, Philip is left dumbfoundedly believing that they belong to his wife's lover while we realise that both Philip and Greg have been betrayed by the elusive Ginny.

Ayckbourn was consciously trying to write a well-made play: 'I think this is important for a playwright to do at least once in his life since, as in any science, he cannot begin to shatter theatrical convention or break golden rules until he is reasonably sure in himself what they are and how they were arrived at'. In fact he is relying on a long tradition of comic misunderstanding. There is a very strong echo of *The Importance of Being Earnest* in the way one character, at the end of the first scene, rashly decides to pursue another to the country: just as Algernon scribbles down on his shirt cuff Jack Worthing's address – The Manor House, Woolton, Hertfordshire – so Greg here picks up the cigarette packet proclaiming The Willows, Lower Pendon, Bucks. In Wilde this leads to one of the great entrances in all comedy with Jack Worthing arriving in mourning for a brother who has already turned up. The key difference is that Wilde clears up the misunderstanding in five minutes whereas Ayckbourn makes Greg's confusion about parents and lovers the substance of the whole play.

Coward (a writer Ayckbourn admires) also made use of

the prolonged-misunderstanding joke in his 1936 one-acter, *Hands Across The Sea*. In that play a rather dim couple from a Malayan rubber plantation, the Wadhursts, turn up at a swish Mayfair cocktail party thrown by a Mountbattenish couple and are assumed to be two entirely different people from way out East, the Rawlinsons. Although Coward's play is very funny, it depends much more on the author's Bohemian joy in showing rampant egoists running rings round their guests than on any great technical ingenuity. Coward also keeps the situation afloat for 40 minutes: not for a couple of acts.

To some people, of course, Ayckbourn's technical ingenuity is itself suspect. John Russell Taylor in an interesting review of *Relatively Speaking* in *Plays and Players* (June 1967) says the play depends on obvious falsities: 'When Greg arrives at The Willows he is made to behave as surely no young man in the world would behave, and certainly no-one as shy and self-conscious as he would, by marching in and not introducing himself at all (not even "I'm Greg – Ginny's fiancé") and remaining sublimely unconscious of the total mystification his arrival causes. Why? Obviously, because the play would stop there and then if he were permitted to say more.'

Precisely what makes the play fascinating, however, is the way Ayckbourn, making a great leap forward as a dramatist, maintains a delicate balance between technical cleverness and psychological probability. The play is both an exquisite conjuring trick and something based in a kind of human truth, however theatrically magnified. In the very first scene Ayckbourn plants the idea that Greg is naïve, credulous, a virgin until he met Ginny and someone who is panicky about his own identity: he claims that his first action on waking in the morning is to fish under his bed for his slippers to make sure that he knows who he is.

What more natural than that someone so insecure should not march boldly into a house and proclaim his identity but enter tentatively and conduct his conversation through a series of evasions?

John Russell Taylor also finds falsity in the scene in which Sheila and Greg first meet without each discovering who the other is. But things like this do happen. I can vividly recall arriving, with a group of showbiz guests, rather prematurely at what we assumed to be an eve-of-Tony-Awards party at Sardi's in New York: it took us an agonisingly long time, and a whole series of cross-purpose conversations, to realise that we had stumbled into a private birthday celebration on the wrong floor. As in *Mr Whatnot*, where everyone thinks someone else has invited the hero, Ayckbourn also plays on a very English phenomenon: the nervousness of the guest encounters the inbred politeness of the host. Particularly as played by Celia Johnson and Richard Briers in the West End production, the initial scene of confrontation acquired almost Pinteresque overtones: the pauses got longer and longer as her bulging-eyed desperation met his impenetrable mystery. This was funny. And funny because true. In England we are still so wary of direct statement it would be just possible to walk into a Bucks house on a Sunday morning and be given a drink on the assumption that one was acquainted with someone living there.

Watching or reading the play, one is constantly caught between two emotions: delight in what Coleridge called a 'playwith', a mechanically ingenious toy, and admiration for the way Ayckbourn psychologically motivates the misunderstandings: not merely through Greg's naïvete but also through Philip's treatment of his wife as if she were a second-hand car and through Sheila's attempt to foster her husband's suspicions by having special letters delivered to her on a Sunday morning. Machinery alone never makes one laugh. The play's complexities only work *because* Philip is unfaithful, *because* Sheila is trying to foster his jealousy and *because* the communication gap between them is so large that a total stranger can pass through it virtually undetected.

Ayckbourn also very subtly uses the vertiginous complexities and comic role-playing to reveal the truth about the marriage of Philip and Sheila. Greg, who still believes he is talking to his fiancée's parents, starts to tell them about Ginny's past *affaire* with a married man. Philip, still playing the role of Ginny's father, finds himself having to defend the behaviour of the married man (himself). Sheila, cast unwillingly in the role of mother, finds herself attacking it:

SHEILA: Poor girl. Did you hear that, Philip? Poor girl.

PHILIP: Yes. I was just going to say that there were probably two sides.

SHEILA: Nothing but selfishness on his, I should think.

PHILIP: I don't know.

SHEILA: I do.

PHILIP: How do you mean?

SHEILA: It's obvious. I mean, what could he offer her?

PHILIP: It depends on what sort of man he was.

SHEILA: I can't see that that makes an awful lot of difference.

PHILIP: If he was, say, for instance, a rather remarkable man.

SHEILA: If he was all that remarkable, he wouldn't be carrying on behind his wife's back, would he?

PHILIP: Unless he had a singularly unremarkable wife.

SHEILA: Probably his fault if she was. Presumably he was quite happy with her when he married her.

PHILIP: Perhaps she proved a bit of a disappointment though. Pretended to be something she wasn't and turned out quite different.

SHEILA: He probably did the same to her.

PHILIP: That's possible.

By any standards, this is first-rate dramatic irony. Philip is discussing their marriage directly: Sheila quite indirectly. But both are disclosing obliquely their real feelings about each other. Ayckbourn, on the whole an observer of human frailty rather than a conscious moralist, comes close to judging Philip as a selfish, philandering prig. Ayckbourn is not, as his later work proves, puritanically hostile to adultery, merely to the egoistic exploitation of one human being by another.

Ayckbourn himself says of this play that 'character plays a fairly secondary role in it'. Not even the best-oiled comic machine can function, however, without characterisation: Feydeau's spring-heeled adulterers, for instance, are propelled by recognisable lust, greed and panic. One of the marvels of this play is that all the misunderstandings stem from some recognisable traits. Philip is just sufficiently suspicious of his wife's putative lover, Sheila is just sufficiently vague in an upper-middle-class kind of way, Greg is just sufficiently unworldly for their behaviour to have an unforced plausibility. And Ginny is just enough of a liar to set the whole plot spinning. She lies about the phone calls, the flowers, the chocolates, the address on the cigarette packet and thereby gives all that follows a dotty logic. Indeed for Ayckbourn, building on the farcical complexities of *The Square Cat* and the notion of a stranger sucked into an alien household of *Mr Whatnot*, the play represents a major advance into theatrical maturity. It is an elegant construct, a delightful

Fabergé egg of a play; yet it also suggests that the distinctive sound of a middle-class English Sunday morning is that of a marriage quietly falling apart. The play may have been written to give Scarborough holidaymakers somewhere to go in the dry; but it also proved Ayckbourn could write a well-made play based on observable truth.

'The Sparrow'

Marriage is also viewed rather sourly in Ayckbourn's next play, *The Sparrow*, which had a three-week run at the Library Theatre, Scarborough, in July 1967 and which has never resurfaced since. Producer Peter Bridge and director Nigel Patrick, responsible for staging *Relatively Speaking* in the West End, apparently rushed up to Scarborough to see it and then rushed back again as fast as they could. In a sense one can see why. Ayckbourn, having been acclaimed as the new comic saviour the West End was waiting for, had written a rueful comedy about four young people enacting various power games in a grotty flat. It was closer to the world of Ann Jellicoe, Harold Pinter and Charles Dyer than that of Noel Coward. But, although the play has one crucial flaw, it deserved a longer life: to the student of Ayckbourn, it is also a fascinating reminder that he is no boulevard lightweight but an obsessive writer repeatedly returning to the impact of marriage on human relationships.

The charge made against the play at the time was that it was a bit like *The Knack*. It shows us two men competing for the favours of a girl in slightly tacky surroundings. But Ayckbourn had not seen Ann Jellicoe's play when he wrote *The Sparrow*; and, as James Agate once definitively said, if a man turned up with a novel about a rotund, bespectacled bachelor who formed his own club and got erroneously involved in a breach-of-promise case, one would assume not that he had read *Pickwick Papers* but that he had not. I assume that Ayckbourn, who in his job as a BBC drama producer was exposed to a lot of plays, was merely subconsciously offering his own variation on the kind of themes that were floating around English drama, and life, in the 1960s: themes to do with territory, domination and domestic power being aired not only in plays by Pinter and Jellicoe but in the anthropological works of Robert Ardrey and Konrad Lorenz. The play is also definably Ayckbourn's in its disenchanted view of marriage and in its sympathy for the victims of marital power games who finally strike a blow for independence. Ayckbourn is fascinated by the relationship between the exploiter and the exploited; and, from first to last, he is emphatically on the side of the underdog.

What is intriguing about *The Sparrow*, a straight narrative devoid of technical high jinks, is that it only gradually reveals its hand. At first it looks as if we might be in for one of those very English sex comedies, on the lines of *Rattle of a Simple Man*, in which a male virgin fails to make it in the sack with a sexually experienced woman, as we see Ed, a mild little bus conductor with a passion for boat-building, bringing the drenched, mini-skirted Evie back to his squalid flat after a night at the local ballroom. But, after a good deal of comic sparring, the tone changes with the arrival of Tony who owns the flat and who is everything Ed is not: smooth, brutal, authoritative with something of the style of one of Pinter's flash *arrivistes*. Tony Pinterishly treats Evie as if she were a scrubber; and, insisting on his territorial rights, grudgingly allows her to spend the night sleeping in the bathroom.

What follows in the next two scenes is a traditional

sexual takeover. Tony hires Evie as a secretary for the wholesale business he claims to run from his home; and even when Julia, Tony's estranged wife, turns up and eventually reveals that Tony actually sells second-hand cars in a local garage ('He's really very good', says Julia, 'he even overcharged me for mine') Evie remains obstinately committed to being the power behind Tony's throne and turning his squalid little pad into a hyper-efficient office. Having switched her affections, she is even quite happy to see the boat-building, bus-conducting Ed move out lock, stock and paddle.

In the final scene, the real nature of the power struggle becomes clear. We learn that Tony has all this while been getting his revenge on the hapless Ed who once had a roll in the hay with Julia after a marital bust-up (Julia has always claimed Ed seduced her). We also see Tony passionately re-united with Julia and no longer needing Evie as a sexual weapon. So Evie and Ed, the two pawns in a complex marital game, join forces and move out. Ed plans to give up bus-conducting for boat-building; and Evie will now have the chance to steer him to success. After their experience at the hands of Tony and Julia, they emphatically agree not to get married; and, as the curtain falls, Tony and Julia are once more calling on Ed to arbitrate in yet another marital dispute. But Ed has gone: the umpire, you might say, strikes back.

The one serious flaw in the play (rare in Ayckbourn) is that he wrenches human behaviour in accordance with the demands of his theme. You see this in the character of Evie who begins the play as a funny, chirpy, sparky lady quite sharp enough to see that Ed is a spineless chump being pushed around by a domineering berk who claims to be his friend. But having created a plausible female who makes up in wit what she lacks in instant sex appeal, Ayckbourn then turns Evie into a gullible idiot who swallows all Tony's suspiciously smooth executive chat. There seems not the slightest reason why Evie, on the promise of twenty-five quid and a contract, should sit down on a Sunday morning and type letters in the midst of unhygienic squalor. The only motivation that Ayckbourn really offers is that Evie, who has made little of her own life and who is not really a qualified typist, has an envy of people with a driving powerhouse ambition (she talks nostalgically of going out with a boy with a dynamic urge to be a landscape gardener). The assumption is that Evie can compensate for her own failures by being the woman behind a successful man. But by transforming her from a cool cucumber to a dim chit who succumbs to Tony's bombast, Ayckbourn sells the character short.

What makes *The Sparrow* fascinating is what it has in common with other plays of the 1960s and what it tells us about Ayckbourn in particular. Ayckbourn was not (any more than another dramatist) an island; and it is in no way surprising that one should detect echoes of other plays. The shy guy who finds himself upstaged by a fly-man-of-the-world sparks off memories of *The Knack* (1961) and Peter Shaffer's *The Private Ear* (1962). The way Evie is, for a time, magnetically drawn to the strongest man around carries faint echoes of *The Homecoming* (1965). When Tony brings back Julia and throws out Evie, he is falling back on rights of ownership as brutally as Mick in *The Caretaker* (1960). To say this is not to accuse Ayckbourn of carbon-copying: merely to reflect that the 1960s was a period in which many dramatists were preoccupied with the way primitive, animal instincts towards domination were being privately enacted.

What makes the play significant, in terms of Ayckbourn's development, is its harsh, realistic, entirely credible portrait of a modern marriage. Oscar Wilde knew that in married life three's company, two's none; and Tony and Julia are portrayed as the kind of warring, sloppy, sexy, erratic couple whose union is precariously sustained both by the need for an audience and by the presence of someone whom they can utilise, bully and employ as punch bag, **confidant** and tool. Ayckbourn takes sex and violence off **the streets** and puts it back in marriage where it belongs; and shows how this kind of alliance always needs a buffer state. In this case, Ed, who explains to Evie how he got involved:

ED: . . . Anyway, one night they had one of their punch-ups. They didn't half have some punch-ups. She used to sling the lot at him – plates, cups, chairs – the lot. And usually it used to finish with him landing her one and then there was quiet again and after about five minutes I'd come out of my room and there they'd be snogging away in front of the television – until she smashed that. . . .

EVIE: Just like my Mum and Dad – blow for blow the same. You know, my Mum spent more time in the Marriage Advice Bureau than she did at home.

ED: Anyway, one night he didn't take a swing at her as usual, he just went out on the booze. Didn't come back till the next evening. And there I am in my room working on the canoe, cutting a mortice and tenon, when she comes flying in saying 'Oh Ed, Ed – it's all over Ed'. Things like that. Before I know what's happening we're rolling all over the floor and she's kissing me and I'm saying, you know – 'What's the matter then?' and she just keeps saying 'Oh Ed, Ed' and she's that violent we keep nearly crashing against the boat. . . .

There is even a touch here of Jimmy, Alison and Cliff from *Look Back In Anger*. What makes Ayckbourn's play different is that he shows the manipulated can join forces and mutiny, the boat-builders can come out of the closet and the meek can inherit the earth. At the end, as Tony and Julia noisily shout for Ed to come to their rescue, the door finally slams.

It is a pity that Peter Bridge and Nigel Patrick hurried back to London quite so quickly after seeing *The Sparrow* in Scarborough; for it is a vital missing link in Ayckbourn's treatment of marriage. In *The Square Cat* he showed a repressed wife and mother, after an abortive encounter with a pop star, returning to worship the Home Counties *penates*. In *Relatively Speaking* he showed an upper-middle-class wife rumbling her husband's adultery and sowing some troubling doubts in his own mind. Now in *The Sparrow* he depicts a shy man and a plain girl escaping the fetters of matrimony. The play is a bit schematic. It has none of Ayckbourn's technical hoopla to sweeten the pill. But it shows him wrestling with the omnivorous nature of wedlock and proving, with signal optimism, that the sparrow does not automatically have to be consumed by the big birds of prey.

'How The Other Half Loves'

With Ayckbourn's next major play, *How The Other Half Loves* (first seen in Scarborough in July 1969 and at the Lyric Theatre, London, in August 1970) theme and technique inexorably mesh. Everyone remembers it, I suspect, as the 'dinner-party play': the one in which a couple of timorous guests are seen dining simultaneously in two different households *on successive evenings*. But that is only one scene in a brilliant play that also deals with class, sex, marital discord, individual rebellion and the nature of deception. The dazzling technique is not there as an end in itself but to service an idea; and one indicated by the punning title which obliquely refers both to one's marital partner and the class system. The play is very much about different styles of loving amongst the employers and the employed.

Initially the true nature of the play was somewhat obscured in London by Robert Morley's idiosyncratic star performance. Ayckbourn is basically an ensemble writer: his work needs to be performed either by a permanent company (as at Scarborough) or by stars of equal weight. When Peter Bridge cast Robert Morley in the role of Frank Foster in the initial London production, the play inevitably changed its character. Morley is a natural life- and stage-enhancer. So a play about three married couples inevitably became a work dominated by Morley's own lustrous charisma. If Ayckbourn silently chafed at the regality of the star system, he at least picked up some very handsome royalties since the show ran for 869 performances and confirmed his position as the West End's hit-man.

The play's initial conceit is beautifully blithe. It puts two living rooms, belonging to two different couples, on to the same stage. But where any normal dramatist would place them side by side in the conventional manner, Ayckbourn superimposes one on top of another. Thus the upper-middle-class living room occupied by the Fosters occupies exactly the same space as the middle-middle-class room dwelt in by the Phillipses. So entwined are the two sets that the communal settee has smart cushions belonging to the Fosters and slightly tattier ones owned by the Phillipses. Obviously the comic possibilities of this juxtaposition are enormous with characters leading separate emotional and physical lives while brushing up against each other. But it also highlights the basic theme of the play: the way sexual attitudes are conditioned by class. It is not merely a device. It is also a practical demonstration of a theme.

What also makes the play fascinating is Ayckbourn's highly sophisticated use of time as well as place. In the first scene both the Fosters and the Phillipses are in the middle of the breakfast rush; but there seems to be a miniscule difference in the time at which the events are happening. In the second scene Ayckbourn constructs the famous dinner-party episode (eat your heart out Goldoni) in which two different events on a Thursday and Friday evening are collapsed into one. Beyond that, Ayckbourn also later shows a character rushing out of one house and arriving at the other almost simultaneously, throwing all notions of time and place into surreal confusion. I can think of no-one before Ayckbourn in dramatic history who has done this. Shakespeare (most notably in *Othello*) concertina'ed events into a 'stage time' different from real time. Pirandello confused past and present. J. B. Priestley in his 1930s time plays questioned the notion of sequential, chronological time while always sticking within the cosy framework of stage convention. Ayckbourn (without being a Shakespeare or a Pirandello) breaks all the rules of theatre, however, by simultaneously showing us two different events on two different nights in two different places. That is supreme technical virtuosity. But what matters is that he shatters the conventional rules without losing sight of his fundamental comic purpose.

What exactly is that comic purpose? Part of it is immediately established in the first scene with the class contrasts between the Foster and Phillips households. The Fosters, an apparently childless, well-to-do-couple, lead good-tempered lives in which even the wife's coming home drunk at two in the morning is not something enquired into too rigorously. The Phillipses, on the other hand, are messy, rancorous and typically middle-class with the socially-concerned wife endlessly filing articles from the *Guardian* and the husband snappishly objecting to peanut-butter sandwiches for breakfast. With the Fosters the great crisis is running out of bathroom stationery and the electric toothbrush going on the blink: with the Phillipses, it's baby Benjamin trying to swallow a spoon and toy-squeakers getting stuck in people's shoes. But Ayckbourn is not simply making easy sociological points. He is suggesting (or rather demonstrating) that class dictates the tone and style of behaviour. Take, for instance, the way Teresa Phillips, edgily querulous, brings up the question of husband Bob's absence the previous night:

> TERESA: Did you want some breakfast then? Is that what this is all about?
> BOB: Not if – you're rushed off your feet.
> TERESA: Well, there's no need to go on at me. I mean considering the fact that you rolled in here at two o'clock this morning stinking drunk and I haven't said a word about it –
> BOB: Till now –
> TERESA: Haven't said a word about it, I think it's really a bit of a nerve to sit there complaining there isn't any breakfast –
> BOB: I'm not complaining.
> TERESA: Good.

Meanwhile, over at the Fosters, Frank brings up the question of his wife Fiona's late arrival the previous night in very different style:

> FRANK: Where did you get to then?

34

FIONA: When?
FRANK: Last night?
FIONA: Oh, I got held up –
FRANK: Oh. (*Pause.*) I see. Doesn't matter.
FIONA: It's no secret. There's no secret about it.
FRANK: Isn't there?
FIONA: No. No secret at all.
FRANK: Good.
FIONA: More coffee.
FRANK: Ah, thank you.

Not only are the Fosters Pinteresquely evasive where the Phillipses are rudely blunt. Ayckbourn also makes the point throughout the scene that adultery – or at least nocturnal absence – means different things in different households. Fiona's life consists of meetings, engagements, 'dashing around' as she euphemistically puts it: her husband is even moodily reconciled to having spent their wedding anniversary alone watching television. Fiona has a world outside the house of which adultery forms an unsurprising part. Teresa, on the other hand, finds herself the victim of adultery precisely because she is a classic house-bound, child-ridden wife:

TERESA: No, I'm sick of this. Other husbands tell their wives where they go to. They don't just disappear and come blundering in at two o'clock in the morning. Other husbands – . I mean here I am stuck here with Benjamin and you're out having parties and God knows what else while I'm stuck here.

Ayckbourn is not a didactic writer or pulpit moralist. But there is, for all that, an instinctive sympathy with the harassed wife trying to cope with a prune-covered child and an errant husband and an equally clear dislike of the kind of upper-middle-class wife who skedaddles off on an anniversary and cannot disguise the fact that her husband has bought her the wrong perfume. As in *Relatively Speaking* and *The Sparrow*, Ayckbourn shows himself against emotional exploitation in any form. There is also something implicitly healthier about a house like the Phillipses, in which dirty linen is brandished as well as washed in public, than that of the Fosters in which it would doubtless be sent to the cleaners. The two households are linked by sex (in that Fiona Foster's night out has been spent with Bob Phillips). But they are separated by a whole world of emotional candour.

So what Ayckbourn does in this lengthy and elaborate first scene is not merely establish two different marriages, houses and classes. He also gets the motor of the plot going. Frank Foster, who is Bob's employer, rings him up to ask him if he knows anything about William Featherstone – 'bright little chap from accounts'. Bob, the name implanted in his brain, uses Featherstone as his alibi for the previous night, saying he was advising him about his wife's adultery. Meanwhile Fiona uses Mary Featherstone (whom she hardly knows) as *her* alibi, claiming she was consoling her for an *affaire* William is having. So an entirely innocent couple are dragged into Bob and Fiona's sexual escapade: what is more, a couple whom Frank Foster has invited to dinner that night (Friday). The stage is set.

All good comedy, in the end, is about the meshing of plot and character. And *How The Other Half Loves* – which could easily have been an arid technical exercise – becomes hilarious precisely because the couple invited to dinner are in themselves so bizarre: William is the bullying,

36

upwardly mobile little thruster (beautifully played by Brian Miller in the London production) and Mary the cowed, socially nervous wife whom her husband treats as a do-it-yourself appendage. They are the third example of marriage Ayckbourn gives us in the play; and one locked together in almost sado-masochistic union. At the same time, the hapless Featherstones find themselves playing different roles at the different dinner parties in the play's mountingly lunatic second scene. When they are with the Fosters, they are scarified dependents with William, at one point, mistaking his boss's gesture in placing his shoe on the table and offering to tie up his laces. When they are with the Phillipses, they become embroiled in a full-frontal domestic row in which plates, beer cans and insults are hurled about in wild profusion. It is a famous scene which people think is funny because it shows two people in swivel chairs – which swing through an angle of 90 degrees – pretending to be at two distinct dinner parties. I suspect it is funny because of who the people are and the roles they are forced to play: with the Phillipses they aim to be marital mediators and Mr Featherstone ends up with the contents of a soup tureen flung in his face; and with the Fosters they aim to make a cool impression only for Mr F. to wind up sitting under a lavatorial drip. All of which suggests that comic 'business' is never funny in isolation: it all depends on who is doing it and whom it happens to.

Admittedly in the second act the fun becomes a little more mechanical and 'plotty': in the first scene Frank Foster jumps, on rather shaky evidence, to the conclusion that Bob Phillips is having an *affaire* with Mary Featherstone and, as a result, William Featherstone goes charging round to the Phillips house clutching a monkey-wrench to administer physical retribution. But, even when the dynamics of farce take over, Ayckbourn does not squander his sense of character or theme. William Featherstone's cry 'Do you realise, Mrs Foster, the hours I've put into that woman' is one of the most chilling and funny in all Ayckbourn: a terrifying lower-middle-class conception of a wife as some kind of vacuum one fills up with hobbies and leisure pursuits. Ayckbourn men seem to treat their women either with cool, sublime indifference; or as bits of do-it-yourself apparatus with which they tinker obsessively during their spare time.

If Ayckbourn sees the ridiculousness of such figures, he also is aware of the danger of the benign meddler. I once dubbed Ayckbourn 'Scarborough's Ibsen'. One reason was that, exactly like the Ibsen of *The Wild Duck*, he is constantly alert to the harm done by bumbling interventionists who try to chip away the scales from other people's eyes. Ibsen handles the theme tragically: Ayckbourn comically. Frank Foster in this play becomes a suburban Gregers Werle precipitating disaster by telling people what he sees as uncomfortable truths. He informs the loony Featherstone that his wife is involved in some grand passion and so triggers off all kinds of domestic violence. 'They were perfectly happy until you started on them', his wife tells him; and it is quite true that his paternalist attitude to his employees' lives is a source of mayhem.

In the final scene Ayckbourn brings the various strands of the play together. Frank Foster has everyone round to his house for a Sunday-morning air-clearing session and sorts out the various issues he himself has complicated. William is forced to utter an inarticulate apology to his innocent wife ('It's difficult for him', says Mary. 'He's never been wrong before, you see'). Bob and Teresa, who have made their peace in bed, are publicly reconciled. And

Fiona finally confesses to Frank that she has had a casual fling: something that can apparently be put right with dinner and a bottle of wine. But there is a teasing hint at the end that Frank and Teresa, who have been decisively tromped, may get something together and give the sexual merry-go-round a further nudge in the right (or perhaps the wrong) direction.

In cold prose, it is hard to do justice to the play's overpowering image: the cheek-by-jowl juxtaposition of two families. In the theatre one is constantly obliged to compare and contrast the neat, smart, emotionally evasive Fosters and their well-oiled routine with the scruffy, slobby, emotionally hectic Phillipses and their life of eruptive chaos. Caught between them in a kind of no-man's-land are the unfortunate Featherstones who are variously alibis, guests, victims and aggressors. Obviously the play is written to amuse and entertain and to give the spectator a good night out. But, under and through its technical finesse, it is saying something of general concern: that attitudes to love and sex are tied up with class and environment. At the Foster end of the social scale you protect yourself against any possible hurt with a studied, formal indifference ('If for some reason', says Frank to his wife, 'you were doing something on Wednesday night that you didn't want me to know about, fair enough. No business of mine'). At the Phillips end, you fling the cutlery outside the front door, chase each other round the dining-room table in front of guests but you patch up your differences instantly between the sheets. Ayckbourn, permanently preoccupied with marriage, here extends and develops his treatment of it by showing the different ways of treating adulterous flings: with benign neglect, angry retaliation, do-gooding interference. How you react, he suggests in this thoughtful romp, is likely to depend on such staples of English life as class, income, education and emotional training.

Although still working as a BBC drama producer in Leeds, Ayckbourn was now beginning to establish that reputation for industry that delights audiences, annoys critics and makes the lives of commentators difficult. In the same year as *How The Other Half Loves* first saw the light of day in Scarborough (1969), he also came up with a couple of briefer works. *Ernie's Incredible Illucinations* was a one-act children's play about an adolescent Billy Liar whose spiralling fantasies involve his parents, his auntie and even the doctor to whom he is sent to be cured: it is a pleasant, much-performed work which Ayckbourn himself regards as 'a starting-point for imaginative games'.

Also in 1969 came *Countdown*, a short duologue first performed at Hampstead Theatre Club as part of *Mixed Doubles*, an entertainment on marriage. None of the other writers (including Harold Pinter, James Saunders, Alun Owen and George Melly) took a particularly optimistic view of the institution. Ayckbourn's contribution, consisting of a conversation that takes place 'any evening in any week in any year of this twenty-two year old marriage' was the bleakest by far. The banal, muted pleasantries, as the wife brings in a pot of tea on a tray, are counterpointed by the characters' innermost thoughts which are here articulated. It is not a new technique: O'Neill used it throughout the whole of *Strange Interlude* to faintly wearying effect. But it does point up the characters' failure to communicate with each other, the intensity of their locked-in antipathies and the idea that the shared laughter of courtship gives way over the years to the strained bitterness of marriage. A character in Hugh Leonard's play, *Da*, defines marriage as 'the maximum of solitude with the minimum of privacy'. That seems to be Ayckbourn's view in this hermetic, cynical duologue: at this juncture, the most pessimistic piece he had committed to paper with none of his usual contrapuntal gaiety.

'The Story So Far'

The notion of Ayckbourn – who now had two West End hits to his credit – as some kind of inexhaustible goldmine received a slight knock with his next play which has had four different productions, three separate title changes but which has never made it to Shaftesbury Avenue or entered the revolving Ayckbourn repertory. It began its life at the Library Theatre, Scarborough, in August 1970 as *The Story So Far*. It started a pre-London tour in August 1971 under the direction of Robin Midgley. It had a second pre-London tour in March 1972 in a revised version under the title of *Me Times Me Times Me* directed by Basil Coleman. Finally it made it, in a very funny production by Sam Walters, to the Orange Tree, Richmond, in November 1978 under the title of *Family Circles*. Reviewing it then, I described it as 'not one of Ayckbourn's best plays but one of his most fascinating'. It proved that Ayckbourn possesses what is probably the most agile and inventive brain ever applied to the creation of comedy in this country. But it also showed there is a point when technical wizardry becomes self-defeating and stifles rather than releases audience laughter.

The play begins deceptively simply. Three strongly contrasted daughters return to the family home for a parental wedding anniversary, rather in the manner of the three sons coming back to the family pad in David Storey's *In Celebration*. The difference is that the three girls all have partners in tow. Jenny, 'thick as a Portuguese gangplank' according to her Dad and palpably pregnant, is married to Oliver, an amiable stuffed shirt with an annoying habit of clicking his fingers. Deirdre, the ebullient, unmarried extrovert, comes touting a willowy young man in shorts called James. And Polly, a fire-breathing, mother-hating virago, is shackled to a pill-pushing, tartan-capped neurotic, David. Casually someone quotes their father's dictum that 'we all marry the wrong people really and there's not much we can do about it'. But, this being an Ayckbourn play, there is everything you can do about it. What he, in fact, does over the next three scenes is to interweave two complex ideas: a fantasy about what might happen if each of the sisters swapped male partners and a family quest to discover if the mother and father are, as everyone suspects, surreptitiously trying to kill each other. It is a breathtakingly clever conceit that brings out all Ayckbourn's ebullient pessimism (however you deal the cards, people still end up with a disastrous marital hand) and leads to some hilarious personality collisions before finally disappearing up its own ingenuity.

What other dramatists find difficult, Ayckbourn handles with apparent ease: exposition, character differentiation, the relation of incident to people. Minor dramatists describe their characters: Ayckbourn reveals them through action. Thus it would be the feckless Deirdre who, having arrived without a present, offers her father a bunch of flowers culled from his own lovingly tended garden. And it would be the tempestuous, mother-loathing Polly, who gets a letter from a neighbour alleging that the father, Edward, is trying to kill the mother, Emma: even the reading of the letter becomes a revelation of malodorous sisterly feelings:

JENNY: She's got to be protected from that man. It's a fine thing when one's own mother isn't safe in her own house.

POLLY: Or put it another way. It's a fine thing when one's own father is reduced to trying to murder his wife out of sheer desperation.

DAVID: You're not saying that this is mother's fault.

POLLY: Of course it is. If he's trying to kill her off, she's no-one to blame but herself. It's just his way of saying thank you for years of utterly miserable marriage.

DEIRDRE: Bloody hell. Isn't she marvellous?

JENNY: This is absolutely outrageous. I won't listen to this. How can you be so disloyal to mother?

POLLY: Or you to father.

JENNY: He's virtually a murderer.

POLLY: He's a long-term victim of that stupid bitch in the kitchen.

By the end of the first scene you know who these people are, the nature of their misalliance, their attitude to their parents, as well as having the feeling of stormclouds gathering ominously over suburbia.

Ayckbourn's ability to *demonstrate* his ideas rather than *discuss* them is shown by the way he swaps the partners around: simply through a change of costume, he makes the point that even a change in material circumstances does not alter the sisters' hereditary traits or the psychological cross they have to bear. Indeed if the play proves anything it is that Philip Larkin was right when he wrote that 'They fuck you up, your Mum and Dad – they may not mean to but they do'; for it soon becomes clear that the three sisters, Jenny, Deirdre and Polly, owe much of their twitchiness to an odd parental alliance. Edward either stumps morosely through the house or spends much of his time in brooding solitude:

Emma, on the other hand, is an ineffectual ditherer with a special penchant for making little cakes, Mummy's Delights, which everyone is at great pains to dispose of. We also get a revealing glimpse of the marriage when two of the men corner Emma and ask her if she feels murderously threatened. She confesses that she and Edward had their 'little problems' to start with. Edward did not like women, used to take her on long hikes and not say much, could not bear to sit in the same room with her for any length of time. It is a wan, funny, echoing portrait of an empty marriage: one that both parties have settled into as an unshakeable habit. 'But then', says Emma, 'Edward and I are a perfect example of what I've always said about marriage. It doesn't matter who you are in this life, when you finally get married, it's bound to be to someone you really deserve.'

What is important, though, about *Family Circles* is the way Ayckbourn gives the play a strong dynamic interweaving the anniversary celebration, the suspicion of parental skulduggery and the partner-changing amongst the children. By the first scene of the second act, downright Polly is disastrously wed to obstinate Oliver, Deirdre is entirely swamping and squashing 'damp, dismal, dizzy David' (who has crashed over and fainted in the midst of the anniversary dinner) and Jenny is trying to shake off the dog-like James who wants to stick by her in her heavily pregnant state. Once again, the joy of this particular scene lies in the way Ayckbourn's rooted pessimism is counterpointed by the hilarity of the personality collisions. Nothing in performance is funnier than the mismatch of the drunkenly noisy Deirdre with the neurotic David who, at one point, despairingly cries: 'Other people take their wives out and introduce them to other people. I've seen them do it. I can't do that. I have to hide

– behind potted ferns and coat stands. Waiting for somebody to carry her home – '. This is classic Ayckbourn with all these irritable alliances going their scratchy way against a background of possible murder: Emma makes Edward a milk drink which she insists no-one else touches and which has to be dashed from the lips of Deirdre who promptly passes out; Edward enters with a hacksaw and immediately James crashes off a pair of rickety steps. There are just enough grounds for believing that something untoward is going on to keep the murder motif tinglingly alive.

My own feeling, however, is that in the final scene Ayckbourn blows it: blows it with brilliance but still blows it. What he does is to combine the process of departure with a reprise of all the relationships we have seen in the previous three scenes. As I said of the Orange Tree production, 'It's like watching a man carving angels on pinheads while also riding a unicycle on a high wire: it takes your breath away but who can laugh when they've no breath?' And even when you have the script in front of you with characters labelled Deirdre, Polly, Jenny, I, II and III (same for the men) one's rapt admiration for the ingenuity of it all is tempered by a feeling that Ayckbourn is allowing character to be submerged by plot. One can almost imagine him writing this scene with a model of the set in front of him and little cut-outs of the characters being shunted back and forth as he manipulates the exits and entrances. At his perihelion, Ayckbourn blends pyrotechnics and insight: here, I feel, the tricks take over.

I still think it is a pity that *Family Circles* has never been published or entered the revolving repertory of Ayckbourn's works. It is much too good to languish unseen. By the end of the last frantic, final scene a point has been made: Deirdre I, Polly II and Jenny III have decided to stay behind at the end of the weekend, packing off their respective menfolk, to protect their parents from each other. Edward and Emma, precarious survivors on the marital battlefield, have gone off for a quiet walk leaving their messed-up daughters behind all desperately crying for their Mother and Father on the assumption that murder has finally taken place. As in *How The Other Half Loves* Ayckbourn puts in a plea for non-intervention, suggesting that the best thing we can do, in regard to other people's marriages, is to leave ill alone.

Family Circles instructively proves that there are limits to what farce or comedy can contain; that there comes a point when the audience is so busy working out just who is who that it has no time left to laugh; that the more ingenious the complexity, the greater the danger that the texture of the writing will itself thin out; that the artist's own delight in mechanical complexity can become a self-gratifying game. *Family Circles* is eminently worth reviving because of the insights it offers into Ayckbourn's progressive disenchantment with matrimony and because much of it is ghoulishly and uproariously funny. But I also feel Ayckbourn learned from it that there comes a point when the technical wizardry (if not the kissing) has to stop.

Despite the failure of *Family Circles* (then sailing under the title of *The Story So Far*) to make it into the West End Ayckbourn had by 1970 established an enviable reputation as the commercial theatre's hit-man: a salvation from Scarborough at a time when Shaftesbury Avenue was suffering from creeping inanition. The steady growth through the swinging 1960s of the National Theatre and the Royal Shakespeare Company at the Old Vic and the Aldwych respectively meant that more and more writing, acting and directorial talent was being creamed off by the two subsidised giants. The National Theatre, in particular, had a happy knack of annexing talent (such as that of Peter Nichols who wrote *The National Health* for them) that had had its first major exposure in the West End. Between 1965 and 1970 it is fair to say that the commercial theatre was beginning to feel the pinch of competition from the state-financed companies and that it enjoyed the loyalty of a dwindling band of good writers such as Alan Bennett, Frank Marcus, William Douglas-Home, Anthony Shaffer.

Thus the eruption of Ayckbourn with *Relatively Speaking* was a godsend: here at last was someone who could keep audiences chuckling happily for two hours without insulting their intelligences. But precisely because, with this play and *How The Other Half Loves*, Ayckbourn established himself as a commercial goldmine and a bankable talent it led, I believe, to a serious underestimation of his real worth. Nothing in England arouses more suspicion, particularly amongst the intellectual classes, than popularity. Any dramatist who has the capacity to keep large numbers of people amused or preoccupied is automatically branded as second-rate (witness the consistent smarty-boots denigration over the years of Peter Shaffer). Not only was Ayckbourn popular: he actually wrote comedies, which was further proof that he was Division Two stuff not to be ranked with the big boys like Osborne, Pinter, Arden, Wesker, Storey. I myself blush to recall writing around this time that Ayckbourn's prime achievement was to write dazzling comedies without the safety net of social comment.

I was wrong. Indeed we were all wrong. Because Ayckbourn relied on time-honoured comic devices such as sustained misunderstanding (*Relatively Speaking*), because he rewrote the geography of stage comedy (*How The Other*

Half Loves), we all assumed that he was simply an ingenious manipulator and a skilful comic carpenter with nothing much to say. But a sustained look at his work between 1965 and 1970 shows that he had a number of thematic bees buzzing around his brain: marriage as a form of mutual incomprehension, as a means of colonising third parties, as an institution that subtly varies according to class and the temperament of the partner, plus the notion that well-meaning interference inevitably leads to disaster. Ayckbourn never (or rarely) announces his theses; but he was already a writer with ungovernable obsessions bubbling away under the surface.

I concede that, at the time, it was difficult to gauge just how obsessive he was largely because works like *The Sparrow* and *Family Circles* were not seen by metropolitan theatregoers or critics. Moreover, at a time when drama was undergoing radical changes, the mere sight of a Home Counties patio or a well-furnished living room was enough to brand a writer as a hangover from the gin-and-it, anyone-for-tennis generation. Even a critic as sharp as Helen Dawson, when confronted by *How The Other Half Loves* (*Plays and Players*, October 1970), began her review thus: 'On the evidence so far, Alan Ayckbourn seems to be a witty but reactionary writer, one who is determined to prove that the drawing-room comedy is bombastically alive and that the traditional snob values of class and manners are still healthy and viable fodder for middle-class entertainment'. If it is reactionary to write about middle-class characters, then I suppose Ayckbourn is guilty. But is it really reactionary to suggest that marriage is a dilapidated institution, that it nearly always works in favour of the man, that emotions get more throttled the higher up the income bracket you go? Around the late 1960s and early 1970s feminist writers in Britain were saying no less. And, without wishing to pretend that Ayckbourn was ever some kind of militant firebrand, I would claim that he was dramatising sexual politics while other people were talking about them. He may have worked within the form of middle-class comedy, but, although in his early plays the rattle of the drinks cabinet and the whirr of the motor-mower are never that far away, he never ever as far as I can see subscribes to 'snob values'. Indeed he is a constant critic of such values: something at the time most of us were too blind and theatrically conditioned to see. As he and we advanced into the 1970s, the key question was whether or not the real nature of his peculiar talent would become more readily apparent.

3

Ritual Behaviour

In the 1960s Ayckbourn established himself. In the 1970s he became a theatrical light industry. He left the BBC to become Director of Productions at the Library Theatre-in-the-Round, Scarborough, in 1970; and in the course of the next decade he wrote twelve stage plays, a musical, a late-night revue and a television play. His work inevitably transferred from Scarborough to London from where it travelled all over the world. Three of his stage plays were done on British television. And he himself was constantly arriving smiling on podia to pick up Best Play and Best Comedy Awards. From 1977 on his work also began to be done regularly at the National Theatre in London: the ultimate seal of metropolitan approval.

This prodigious output and constant performance (his work was translated into twenty-four languages) led Ayckbourn to be dubbed, misleadingly, the English Neil Simon. In fact, the two dramatists have little in common other than that they write deceptively serious comedies, make a lot of money and get their work performed in their own theatres. But the differences between them are far more important than the similarities.

Where Simon is a predominantly verbal writer (whose characters nearly all possess a reflex New York-Jewish wit) Ayckbourn is a basically visual dramatist.

Where Simon's people attempt to keep urban neurosis at bay by saying funny things in a downbeat way, Ayckbourn's characters rarely deal in one-line quotes but reveal their quirkiness through behaviour.

Where Simon works basically within the parameters of Broadway comedy which always require a smidgin of uplift, Ayckbourn frequently takes the English farcical-comedy form and stretches it to its limits.

Where Simon's characters are able to change their own destinies, Ayckbourn's are frequently at the mercy of random collisions and chance events.

Where in Simon you are what you say, in Ayckbourn you are what you do.

Where vintage Simon, like *The Odd Couple,* keeps you continuously chuckling, vintage Ayckbourn is much more sierra-like with alternating passages of relative quietness and extended uproar.

But if I had to pinpoint the crucial difference between them, it would be that Ayckbourn is a much more obsessive writer: that he cannot keep away from the destructiveness, the incomprehension, the predatoriness of marriage; the failure of men to understand women; the upward social mobility of Thatcherite private businessmen. If there is one obsession that binds together all his work, however seemingly diverse, it is the notion of human desperation breaking through restrictive social forms. Look at Ayckbourn's work *in toto* and you see that it is about the way we preserve a whole set of rituals – Christmas, family weekends, wedding anniversaries, birthdays, cocktail parties, monogamy even – which bear less and less relation to our actual needs. All drama is a form of sociology; and Ayckbourn, through his craft, is demonstrating what many *New Society* pundits will confirm, which is that our marinated social rituals lack true human content and themselves signal crisis. Being a comic writer, he also shows the incongruity between the form and the content. So *Relatively Speaking* shows sexual duplicity and misunderstanding bubbling away underneath Sunday lunch on the patio and rhododendron-trimming. In *How The Other Half Loves* middle-class marital anger erupts ferociously over dinner, placing the guests in the position of hapless victims and ineffectual spectators. And in *Family Circles* a family reunion for a parental wedding anniversary demonstrates that marriage is often a hazardous lottery in which everyone draws the short straw. Wherever two or three are gathered together for a social purpose, suggests Ayckbourn, then the trouble starts.

'Time and Time Again'

You can see this borne out in *Time and Time Again* which had its summer debut in Scarborough in July 1971 and which appeared at the Comedy Theatre in August 1972 with Tom Courtenay memorably in the lead. For the action begins at a post-funeral tea party in a suburban garden. Graham (dogmatic know-all) and Anna (his clamped-down wife) are giving a little do after the funeral. The party is for Peter, one of Graham's employees who has helped with the funeral arrangements. Peter is a muscular sports fanatic who brings along his delectable fiancée, Joan. And what is clear is that the propriety of the occasion is merely a mask for all kinds of sexual competition. Graham, a born dirty old man, has clearly arranged the tea party so that he can make a pass at Joan. Meanwhile Graham's live-in brother-in-law, Leonard, a moony underachiever who sits in the garden communing with a gnome while the others are all having tea in the conservatory, also gets hooked on Joan. Indeed he accepts Peter's invitation to play cricket with the East Pendon Occasionals purely to get close to her. The mainspring of the plot shows Leonard pinching Peter's girl from him while all the time making him think that Graham is the guilty party. The sexual cockfight that is the play's running theme stems from an occasion intended to pay tribute to the burial of an old woman, Leonard's mother.

It is not, however, simply a wry comedy about vacant rituals. On one level, it is also a play about the absurdity and vanity of masculine competition and an endorsement of the luckless Peter's remark that 'there's more to life than winning trophies'. The three men in the play are all in pursuit of the same woman; and she very sanely abandons all of them. Ayckbourn exposes the dottiness of their behaviour; but suggests that, if you do compete, it is better to be a luckless, accident-prone thickie like Peter or a congenital no-hoper like Leonard than a nasty little thruster like Graham. Ayckbourn, a natural winner of trophies in his chosen field, always displays a humane, likeable and civilised sympathy for life's also-rans. That, however, is the obligatory 'nut of message' which David Hare once suggested all modern dramatists felt obliged to put in their plays. At a deeper level, Ayckbourn is also tackling a theme which he was to develop in later plays: the casual destructiveness of the innocent. This theme is embodied in the fascinating figure of Leonard.

Outwardly Leonard ('a comic suburban Hamlet', Peter Lewis dubbed him in the *Daily Mail*) is harmless, defenceless, naïve: someone who talks to gnomes, quotes poetry and once taught English, History, Religious Instruction and 'had a rather attractive line in nature walks'. But he is also the play's agent of disruption. Within a few minutes of meeting Peter he has, in a spasm of joke sparring, landed him a blow in the stomach. Peter, tinkering with a jammed mower, then gets his fingers stuck in the blades while Leonard pulls the mower gently backwards. When it comes to the marvellous, off-stage cricket match in the second scene, Leonard is no less destructive: in his outsize flannels and undersize boots, he looks helplessly comic, but when fielding he hangs on to the ball while declaring his love for Joan, irritatedly chucks it back in and finds he has hit Peter on the knee.

Emotionally, he is no less the innocent destroyer. His covert *affaire* with Joan reduces Peter to a mooning wreck, turns Graham into a full-time, binocular-toting spy ('He's hardly been to work at all', complains his wife) and ultimately leads Peter into an attempted strangulation of his boss. There is nothing malicious or ill-intentioned about Leonard: he simply produces chaos. It is hard to erase the image of Tom Courtenay, ramshackle, untidy, beguilingly guileless, leaning heavily on collapsible chairs and playing Leonard as someone whose innocence is as dangerous as a minefield. Chekhov once said that women do not like weak men; but they like men with weaknesses. And Leonard certainly has plenty of those.

Time and Time Again shows Ayckbourn getting deeper and deeper into character: it is a sign of his increasing maturity that Leonard's role as an agent of farcical mayhem is combined with a sense of pain and loss. As his brother-in-law never ceases to remind him, he could not even hold on to his wife and three children. It is typical of Leonard's Chekhovian gift for disaster that even his exit from the family home (he left his wife and lover together and then found, after his dignified departure, that he had forgotten his suitcase) was accompanied more by error than towering outrage.

This rich play – with its depleted rituals and Leonard's well-documented dangerous fecklessness – also highlights the hardest of all Ayckbourn's gifts to bring out on the printed page: his visual sense. His plays, as written, are in a sense all blueprints for performance. They simply cry out to be seen because Ayckbourn, a craftsman to his fingertips, makes so many of his points through sight gags.

I found on seeing this play again early in 1981 in a very good production by Nicholas Barter at the Oxford Playhouse, that it was astonishing to witness the pulverising effect of a single joke. In the first scene Leonard and Joan chat in the garden while Graham ferociously stares at them from the vantage point of the conservatory. Simply to annoy his voyeuristic brother-in-law, Leonard persuades Joan to stick her tongue out at him. She does so and Graham, in sheer disbelief, chokes on his sandwich. Not, coldly described on the page, a major piece of comic invention. But it kept the audience laughing for a good half-minute partly because of its sheer improbability (pretty girl sticks out tongue at her boy friend's boss) and partly because it sprang directly from character. It would not be funny if just anyone did it. It was funny here because it sprang from Leonard's mischievousness and Graham's leering nosiness. But it is also a mark of Ayckbourn's technique that he builds on this gag so that, when Leonard and Joan return to the conservatory, Graham wantonly and cruelly brings up the fact that Leonard was once thrown out by his wife, bag and baggage. A chill infects the spring air as, for a moment, Leonard falls uncharacteristically silent.

Alan Ayckbourn

Even Ayckbourn's craftsmanship is not iron-clad. After the painful hilarity of the first act, the second act slightly runs out of invention: Graham's impotent fury at discovering Leonard and Peter playing draughts rather than going for each other's jugular is a weak way to end a scene. Having created bitingly credible characters in Leonard and Graham, Ayckbourn does not do much more than make Joan a seductive beauty and Peter a musclebound chump.

He does, however, score a minor triumph with Anna, Graham's long-suffering, allegedly infertile wife, who talks of fifteen years of coping with marriage with a gentle and quiet despair and who, lacking love, affection and a humane husband, has turned mealtimes into a prolonged sexual and religious ritual. She is one more in Ayckbourn's army of suffering wives but one who is not entirely cowed or defeated. When Graham prattles on about his legendary father – some six-foot-four giant who the day he was born was given a week to live – Anna curtly cuts in with: 'He was an awful old man with loose teeth who kept telling you he was living on borrowed time. . . .'

Anna's quip is, in fact, part of the play's continuous, sidelong assault on a patriarchal, competitive, male-dominated world where figures like Graham (who never had the imagination to talk to an invisible friend as a child) rise to the top and where daffy destroyers like Leonard wind up raking leaves in the municipal park. 'I like to like my people', Ayckbourn once said; and, though he is certainly not an overt moralist, he here vividly shows the fools men make of themselves when (like Graham, Leonard and Peter) they all starting chasing the same girl and indulging in some frenzied machismo race. It is hard to pin the title down to any one specific meaning; but it does suggest to me that there is a cyclical repetition to masculine sexual competition and that it is hard to break the eternal daisy-chain. The play's real advance, however, is that it shows Ayckbourn creating in Leonard a character who has a life before and after the play, who exists in the three dimensions of comedy rather than the two dimensions of farce and whose very passivity and lack of will activate a series of linked mishaps. Leonard is hopeless, inept, fanciful, randy; but also, when the chips and the knickers are down, ruthlessly selfish. It is that fine Chekhovian moral balance that suggests Ayckbourn is never content to repeat a success but is always trying to find ways of making comedy more truthful. He is a pathfinder rather than a comic machine.

'Absurd Person Singular'

Ayckbourn's next play, *Absurd Person Singular* (which had its premiere at Scarborough in June 1972, arrived at the Criterion, London, in July 1973 and which has since put a girdle round about the earth) shows the separate strands of his talent intermeshing. This is the Big One. The one that shows his fascination with the desperation behind English social rituals interlocking with his well-oiled comic craft. Most dramatists seem to start with a set of ideas they wish to convey and gradually master theatrical technique as they go along (David Hare is a classic case of a dramatist whose plays get more polished with time). Because he started so young, Ayckbourn never seemed to have any problem with the clock-making aspect of play-writing. But, as his vision of life has matured, so his plays have got richer. In this one, form and content meet in perfect harmony.

'A play', Kenneth Tynan once wrote, 'is an ordered sequence of events that brings one or more of the people in it to a desperate condition, which it must always explain and should if possible resolve. If the worst that can happen is the hero's being sent down from Oxford, we laugh and the play is a farce; if death is a possibility, we are getting close to tragedy.' But the two forms can miscegnate and Ayckbourn has here written a farcical tragedy (rather like Erdman's *The Suicide*) in which death and destruction are never far away.

Consider. Of its six characters, four stare disaster in the face. We have a philandering architect whose buildings collapse and who faces professional ruin; his screwed-up, suicide-prone wife who has been popping pills since she was eight-years-old; a bank manager last seen living in a frozen Victorian house with a wife whom he does not understand and whom he can barely communicate with; and the wife herself who is a gin-swilling dipso immured in her bedroom. As the title punningly suggests, these are all people who are ridiculous, solitary, unable to cope with the demands of life. The play's two survivors are an unimaginative husband and wife dominated, respectively, by power and by cleanliness.

This is really a play about many things. The provincial pecking order. Male myopia. Empty rituals. Desperation inside marriage. But what gives it theatrical momentum is partly the slightly artificial Dickensian structure whereby the action covers Christmas Past, Christmas Present and Christmas Future and partly the way it shows Sidney and Jane Hopcroft progressing to the top of the heap.

In Act One they are party-givers nervously preparing to entertain bank manager Ronald Brewster-Wright and his wife, Marion, local architect Geoffrey Jackson and his wife Eva plus a hearty, noisy, unseen couple of teachers, Dick and Lottie Potter. Straight off Ayckbourn lets us see that the appalling Sidney plans the party like a military operation, that he views his wife as a kind of social mascot whose prime function is not to let him down and that the Christmas Eve gathering is a go-getting masquerade: theatrically, one of the best strokes is the way Sidney's public, drawing-room laughter abruptly cuts off every time he enters the kitchen.

This first-act party also shows Ayckbourn's skill in doing several things at once. For a start, he establishes the provincial power structure with Brewster-Wright at the top of the heap, Geoffrey Jackson making supplication for him to put in a word on his behalf for the design of a new shopping complex and Sidney, who runs a general stores, wanting to make a bid for the adjoining site:

SIDNEY: But it is a matter of striking while the iron's hot – before it goes off the boil. . . .

RONALD: Mmmmm. . . .

SIDNEY: I mean, in this world, it's dog eat dog, isn't it? No place for sentiment. Not in business. I mean, all right, so on occasions you can scratch mine. I'll scratch yours. . . .

RONALD: Beg your pardon?

SIDNEY: Tit for tat. But when the chips are down it's every man for himself and blow you Jack, I regret to say. . . .

RONALD: Exactly.

Thriftily, Ayckbourn also sketches in characteristics that will become more and more important as the play progresses: Brewster-Wright's upper-middle-class vaguery, Marion's unquenchable gushing and penchant for the gin, Geoffrey's compulsive philandering and chauvinist piggery, Eva's gathering neurosis as, having downed her quota of pills, she tosses the empty glass into the pedal-bin.

On top of this, Ayckbourn also counterpoints Sidney's rabid determination that the party shall further his career with a chain of minor disasters. First, he covers his shirt with fly spray. Then Jane squirts the contents of a soda siphon over Brewster-Wright's trousers. And, finally, donning trilby, mac and wellies, she pops out in the pouring rain to get some tonic water at the off-licence, is locked out of her own kitchen, makes a scurrying, hurried, anonymous entry through the front door and is reduced to spending the rest of the party in the garden because she cannot face her guests. Obviously the idea is blackly funny. But Ayckbourn is not inviting patronising laughter at the expense of lower-middle-class gaucherie. He uses the whole episode to reveal the casual brutality of Sidney towards his wife: as Jane empties her rain-filled wellies into the sink, all Sidney can say by way of support is 'All went off rather satisfactorily anyway. . . .' With consummate skill, Ayckbourn uses the party to demonstrate local hierarchies and personal complexes and to lay dramatic foundations. Sidney's final regret that they never got round to playing party games ('Never mind. Another year.') has, in view of all that is to come, an ironically ominous ring.

The second act, however, is Ayckbourn's masterpiece: another Christmas Eve party, this time at the underprepared Jacksons, in which Eva's suicidal despair pursues its relentless course against a background of domestic chaos and festal celebration. It catches one between wind and water, laughter and tears in exactly the same way as Vanya's attempted shooting of the Professor in *Uncle Vanya*, which for Vanya himself is an expression of accumulated rage but which, for everyone else, is comically absurd. Many great moments of theatre are like this: agonising for the participants, comic for the spectators. But Ayckbourn adds a new gloss by making the Jacksons' guests sublimely unaware of the fact that their hostess is trying to kill herself. A perfect theatrical metaphor for self-encasement.

Eva's private despair is put in the context of a changing balance-of-power in the public world. Sidney Hopcroft is now 'up and coming'. His wife has the social assurance to send back dirty glasses that do not pass her personal Good Housekeeping Test. Meanwhile the philandering Geoffrey Jackson is in trouble with Harrison's Super Shopperdrome, which is costing twice as much as budgeted, and is also being pushed by his wife into hitching his wagon to Hopcroft's rising star. Any dramatist, of course, could do as much. But Ayckbourn's quality is to dramatise his points rather than explain them: thus when everyone descends on the Jacksons' kitchen, in the wake of Eva's suicide bids, to sort out the oven, the sink and the light fitting, it is Hopcroft who bustlingly tries to take charge. There is even a touch of *The Admirable Crichton* about the way the upper-middle-class Brewster-Wright is reduced to baffled impotence when confronted by naked wires dangling from the ceiling, while Hopcroft fetches his tools from the car to cope with the blocked drains.

The core of the act is the way Eva, reduced to dumb despair by her 'sexual flying Dutchman' of a husband, tries to kill herself by leaping off a ledge, running at a kitchen knife, putting her head in the oven, swallowing pills and paint stripper and hanging herself from the light flex. One classic rule of farce is that characters go about their business with a ratty single-mindedness in little pools of solitude: think of the way Feydeau's adulterers are strangely impervious to the humiliations of lust. But Ayckbourn, with great legerdemain, doubles the stakes by

61

having each of the guests single-mindedly pursue his or her fixation. So Jane mistakes Eva's head-in-the-oven for a bungled cleaning attempt and cheerily takes over. Sidney interprets Eva's desperate attempt to retrieve pills that have gone down the drain as a desire to unblock the sink. And Brewster-Wright, in his vague way, thinks that her attempted hanging is part of an urge to do something with the damaged light fitting. Eva's despair is matched by everyone else's blithe, uncomprehending selfishness. As Benedict Nightingale observes in his fine analysis in *An Introduction to 50 Modern British Plays*: 'Mutual incomprehension, the source of so much of Ayckbourn's comedy, is here taken to extremes that a lesser writer might make simply tasteless or cruel. Suicidal despair on the one hand, a genial and kindly imperviousness on the other: the contrast produces a kind of grisly, unnerving hilarity. This is bravura writing.'

By the third bleakly funny act the power reversal and personal incomprehension have reached their apotheosis. Brewster-Wright now sits in his unheated Victorian kitchen on Christmas Eve almost oblivious to the fact that his wife is immured in her room in a permanent alcoholic stupor. The roof has literally fallen in on the super Shopperdrome, almost killing the manager and ruining Geoffrey Jackson's professional reputation. Only Hopcroft the suburban jerry builder and property developer ('Half his tenants', says Jackson, 'are asking to be re-housed and they haven't even moved in yet') is thriving.

Indeed, with great acumen, Ayckbourn demonstrates Hopcroft's growing power lust by the games he wants people to play. In the first act (on home base) he envisages a modest Pass the Parcel and musical bumps. By the second act, he wants to 'get everyone jumping about'. And, by the third act, he and his wife have invaded the

Brewster-Wright's territory, distributed direly unsuitable presents (electrical screwdrivers for 'Ron' who was nearly electrocuted in the second act, a bottle of gin for the pickled Marion) and literally forced the cowering occupants of the house to dance to his particular tune: a Scots reel. Robert Cushman in the *Observer* spoke of 'the forced formality that for me maimed the finale of *Absurd Person Singular*'. I would have said it was artificial (so is the whole play with the same people turning up at each other's houses on successive Christmas Eves) but truthful. Embarrassingly inept hosts in the first act, the Hopcrofts are now in total control. Written at a time when property developers had been given a licence to build, the play became a surreptitious political comment on the withering decline of the professional classes and the rise of the fly, deft, make-money-quick provincial profiteer.

That gives the play its public rhythm. But within that there is a wealth of private desperation. Ayckbourn is wonderfully astute at showing the different varieties of male incomprehension: differing because of class. Sidney Hopcroft (in an echo of *How The Other Half Loves*) translates his wife from faintly embarrassing consort to perfect acolyte: in the final scene she weaves in and out amongst the dancers fixing the forfeits. Geoffrey regards Eva as a useful bit of domestic security while he chases tail around town ('She lives her life to a certain extent: I live mine, do what I like within reason'): he can never quite leave her nor can he ever quite commit himself to her. With Ronald and Marion Brewster-Wright, Ayckbourn gives us a classic case of middle-aged non-communication. He is not the first writer to observe that the average, middle-class, well-educated English male is almost chronically incapable of dealing with the opposite sex. But he shows the consequences with devastating accuracy (two lonely people living at opposite ends of a rambling Victorian house) and catches the hilarious pathos of the bewildered male in one of those very rare confessional speeches he sometimes weaves into his plays and which he here gives to the nonplussed Ronald Brewster-Wright:

> Well – this whole woman business, really. I mean, this may sound ridiculous but I've never to this day known what most women think about anything. Completely closed book to me. I mean, God bless them, what would we do without them. I mean, damn it all, one minute you're having a perfectly good time and the next you suddenly see them there – like some old sports jacket or something – literally beginning to come apart at the seams. Floods of tears, smashing your pots, banging the furniture about. God knows what. Both my wives, God bless them, they've given me a great deal of pleasure over the years but, by God, they've cost me a fortune in fixtures and fittings.

Nothing is sadder than the blocked feelings and blunted sensibility of the public-school English male; Michael Aldridge, with the long, lugubrious features of a bloodhound that has just heard bad news, delivered that speech in Eric Thompson's Criterion production with a wonderful, woebegone puzzlement.

In all this discussion of themes, one tends to take Ayckbourn's technique for granted. But he tells us in his published Preface that he was trying to do something different.

> At that time (1972), I remember, I was becoming increasingly fascinated by the dramatic possibilities of offstage action. Not a new device, granted, but one with plenty of comic potential still waiting to be tapped. Thus

when I came to write *Absurd Person* and started by
setting the action in Jane and Sidney Hopcroft's sitting-
room, I was halfway through the act before I realised
that I was viewing the evening from totally the wrong
perspective. Dick and Lottie were indeed monstrously
overwhelming, hearty and ultimately very boring, and
far better heard occasionally but not seen. By a simple
switch of setting to the kitchen, the problem was all but
solved, adding incidentally far greater comic possibilities
than the sitting-room ever held. . . .

Not only does Ayckbourn turn Dick and Lottie Potter into
a running-gag, a kind of farcical George and Margaret,
who have a vivid identity but no visible presence, he also
adds another powerful, unseen figure in George, the
Jacksons' ferocious monster-dog, who in the second act
confines everyone to the kitchen through his snarling
presence. Typically, Ayckbourn then interweaves the
unseen figures so that George tears a sizeable chunk out of
Dick Potter's leg. It says a lot for Ayckbourn's technical
skill that the incident is as real as if one had actually seen
it.

What makes this play a turning point for Ayckbourn,
however, is the way strong ideas mesh with fully developed
characters. Whenever I read or see the play I think of a
passage in A. Alvarez's study of suicide, *The Savage God*,
in which he describes being overcome with suicidal feelings
on Christmas Eve, phoning his psychotherapist who put
him off until Boxing Day, and taking 45 sleeping pills on
Christmas Day itself. A house-guest brought him a cup of
tea the next morning and assumed that his heavy breathing
was the result of a hangover. 'All my life', says Alvarez, 'I
have hated Christmas: the unnecessary presents and
obligatory cheerfulness, the grinding expense, the anti-

climax.' There is something about the conjunction of Christmas festivity and personal despair that is peculiarly wan: loneliness and depression can be worse at Christmas than at any other time of year. What Alvarez pins down in his confessional, Ayckbourn demonstrates in his play.

Of course, the play makes us laugh. Of course, the play has many of Ayckbourn's characteristic cumulative visual gags (the sight of Jane Hopcroft beating on the glass partition of her own kitchen window in the first act acquires a new resonance in the final act with the Hopcrofts pressing their faces against the Brewster-Wright's backdoor window). But it is also a play in which the laughter winds down rather than up (so much so that some cack-handed Broadway producer wanted to reverse the order of the second and third acts); in which Ayckbourn handles despair more nakedly than ever before; and in which change and decay are perceptibly in the air. As Benedict Nightingale points out: 'The Hopcrofts may have their temporary triumphs and the Evas their respites. The Geoffreys, Marions and Ronalds demonstrate a wider, more general truth. Like everything else in Ayckbourn's bleak, funny world, time itself is deeply inimical to hope, effort, fulfilment and happiness'.

'The Norman Conquests'

Around the time that Ayckbourn's most complex construct to date, *The Norman Conquests*, hit London (it opened at Scarborough Library Theatre in June 1973, Greenwich Theatre in May 1974 and transferred to the Globe in August 1974), one began to detect a faint sniffiness in the air: a feeling that it was about time the chap was put in his place. It is, of course, a characteristic of the English intellectual classes that they cannot bear popularity and success. It takes a writer or painter or composer or performer out of the clutches of the ruling élite and delivers him or her over to the multitude: what is enjoyed by the many must automatically be second-rate (witness the disgraceful treatment given to genre fiction by literary editors, the ritual put-down of Royal Academy Summer Shows by art critics, the active hostility to a dramatist like Peter Shaffer). Ayckbourn, who in 1974 had this trilogy running at the Globe and *Absurd Person Singular* first at the Criterion and then at the Vaudeville, now began to qualify for the treatment.

Not, let me hasten to add, from the drama critics. With the exception of Frank Marcus in the *Sunday Telegraph*, who dubbed *The Norman Conquests* 'a failure', the maligned newspaper reviewers all grasped the point of the plays. But elsewhere one began to detect a feeling that Ayckbourn had been oversold. I reported one such reaction in the *Guardian*: 'I was lunching with a film-critic friend the other day when the conversation turned to Alan Ayckbourn. "You drama critics", said my friend "haven't half made fools of yourselves over Ayckbourn. He's simply a good light-comedy writer yet you and Lambert and Nightingale talk about him as if he were some kind of social and political analyst. I went to see *Absurd Person Singular* and thought it had about as much to say about life as the average *Carry On* movie. Honestly if this is the best the theatre has to offer, then it's in an even worse state than I thought."'

How to answer such a charge? One way is to look at *The Norman Conquests*, which consists of three plays (*Table Manners*, *Living Together*, *Round and Round The Garden*) that cover a traumatic family weekend in a

Victorian country house from 5.30 p.m. on Saturday to 9.0 a.m. on Monday and from the vantage point of three different areas: dining room, living room and garden. Each play makes sense independently; yet only when you put the three plays together do you fully understand what happens during the course of the weekend, comprehend just how blighted and funny-hopeless are all the people on view and grasp the true nature of the pivotal figure of Norman, a libertine assistant librarian who is married to a myopic business-woman, Ruth, proposes a dirty weekend in East Grinstead with his sister-in-law Annie and makes predatory advances towards his other sister-in-law Sarah.

What is initially striking about the trilogy is, of course, its technical cleverness. Ayckbourn combines the 'off-stage' action of *Absurd Person Singular* with the complex sense of time evolved in *How The Other Half Loves* to give us a set of plays not quite like any other. He himself has described how he wrote the plays laterally: 'That is to say, I started with Scene One of *Round and Round The Garden*, then the Scene Ones of the other two plays and so on through the Scene Twos'. But, while writing the plays crosswise, he also gave them a distinct character when viewed downwards. *Table Manners* – with a famous dinner-party scene – has the most frenzy and provokes what B. A. Young called 'an almost unbroken obligato of laughter'. *Living Together* has a slacker pace but explores family relationships in more detail. *Round and Round The Garden* is more conventional, marginally less hilarious but finally exposes the loneliness of the long-distance egoist.

Rather than dwell on the trilogy's technical suavity – since that, in the end, is the least important aspect of it – let me simply provide a few examples of it. Ayckbourn's dovetailing of time and incident is particularly impressive. For instance, chronologically, the sequence begins at

5.30 p.m. with the first scene of *Round and Round The Garden* in which Norman arrives unexpectedly at the rambling Victorian vicarage to whisk Annie off to East Grinstead. The next scene takes place at 6.0 p.m. in the dining room of *Table Manners* where Sarah, who has come down for the weekend with husband Reg to take care of Annie and Reg's demanding bedridden mum, discovers to her horror that Annie is off for a naughty weekend with brother-in-law Norman. With any other dramatist, that in itself would be sufficient complication. But Ayckbourn ends the first scene of *Round and Round the Garden* (it must by now be around 6.25 p.m.) with Sarah triumphantly arriving in the garden to tell Norman that Annie is not going away after all. So, temporally, the scenes overlap; and information gleaned in one scene is used to affect the dramatic development of its predecessor. Not only that: Ayckbourn gives Norman a justifiable despair to motor the first scene of the next play, *Living Together*, which begins in the sitting room at 6.30 p.m.

Ayckbourn is adept at solving problems: 'I thrive', he says, 'when working under a series of pre-conditions, preferably when they are pre-conditions over which I have total control'. He even makes good use of the fact that the actor originally playing Norman was not available for the first few days of the Scarborough season, by giving him a late entrance in one of the plays. But there is nothing admirable about technical ingenuity in itself: what matters is the use to which it is put. Ayckbourn here uses the idea of simultaneous off-stage action to reveal character and get laughs (the two are totally compatible). Thus in the first scene of *Table Manners* the hysterically imperious Sarah despatches her docile husband, Reg, to find out just what Norman and Annie are up to in the living room. And so in the first scene of *Living Together* we have the comic

69

sight of Reg interrupting an emotional *tête-à-tête* between Norman and Annie on the pretext of looking for a wastepaper basket. Simple: but theatrically hilarious. What is more it tells us a lot about the nannying interference, tinged with jealousy, of Sarah and the adaptability of the put-upon Reg.

One could go on multiplying instances. But my real point is that the plays, while enjoyable individually, gain resonance and depth when seen as one gigantic work: a rueful, eight-hour comedy. Why, for instance, is everyone furious with Norman at Sunday breakfast in *Table Manners*? Because, as we learn in Scene Two of *Living Together*, he has made a violent physical attack on the bedridden upstairs Mum; and because, as we discover in Scene Two of *Round and Round The Garden*, he has got paralytically drunk on dandelion wine on Saturday night, failed to bed Annie, excited Sarah's amorous propensities without satisfying them and engaged Reg in a sloshed, loving, near-homosexual embrace. Any one play may look like a jolly romp. Taken together, the three add up to an astonishing picture of fractured rituals (Sarah harps constantly on her wish to sit down just for once to a civilised family meal), personal frustration, marital disharmony and the ruinous legacy of a sexually voracious Mum. This is what the trilogy is actually about.

What is exciting (and little noticed at the time) is that Ayckbourn exposes all this through Norman: a baggy-trousered, woolly-capped, scruffy, dog-like, sexually itchy Peter Pan. Like Leonard in *Time and Time Again* (also played in London by Tom Courtenay) he is a sympathetically viewed bringer of destruction, a havoc-creating Assistant Librarian (judging by this and Kingsley Amis's *That Uncertain Feeling* working on the Dewey System is a great breeder of lust).

Ayckbourn's point is that Norman, agent of chaos, is not some magnetically attractive Don Juan or bronzed Adonis. Norman is a ratbag whose instinctive passion for sexual conquest coincides with a feeling of unhappiness and disappointment in the women he part-seduces. Norman is simply the outlet for all their banked-up frustrations. In the first two minutes of *Table Manners* Ayckbourn gives us a vivid glimpse of Annie's desolate solitude, her slaphappy untidiness, her obligation to stay with her vice-like Mum. Why, asks bossyboots Sarah, does she not tidy up her hair. 'Well', says Annie, 'nobody sees it. The postman, the milkman, couple of cows and Mother.' The house she lives in is later described as 'a very dirty brown museum'. She cannot even leave everyone to fend for themselves because 'I have to explain to them about Mother's pills'. Annie is the eternal coper (every family has one). And she is in a sexual cul-de-sac in which even the lumbering companionship of Tom, a kindly, thick, neighbourhood vet, is better than nothing and in which the prospect of a dirty weekend with Norman in East Grinstead seems like a trip to paradise.

Ayckbourn very skilfully makes Norman the catalyst under the cold lead roof: the readiness of the women in the play to accept his sexual invitations is a mark of their desperation. Nowhere is this better seen than with Sarah whom Ayckbourn slowly reveals to be an emotion-starved wreck. Her husband, Reg, retreats at home into the privacy of his room where he makes toy aeroplanes and invents inscrutably complex games; he forgets the names of his children when he goes to their school; and, moans Sarah, 'it's left to me to explain why you walk straight upstairs as soon as anyone comes to visit us'. Lacking much normal human contact, Sarah overcompensates by treating life as a clockwork routine that has to run smoothly: so much time for dinner, so much time for civilised conversation afterwards.

No-one who saw it will ever forget Penelope Keith's assumption of the role. 'She can rouse the house to hilarity', wrote B. A. Young 'with a straight delivery of a simple line like "I've had a lot of nervous trouble" polishing the dining table as she speaks.' She cleaned the silver as if she wished to do it a personal injury. She flashed panicky smiles at people she particularly detested. She gave a luminous study of a woman who turned table-laying into a Japanese ceremony and whose feelings had for so long been buried under organised domesticity that she greeted Norman's unexpected offer of a weekend in Bournemouth with an unequivocal whoop of delight. The true test of a character is whether you can imagine his or her off-stage life; and between them Mr Ayckbourn and Ms Keith completely conjured up Sarah's world with its bring-and-buy sales, Saturday dancing classes for the kids and twin-set-and-pearled inhibition.

Norman's lust may be the trilogy's activating factor and the litmus paper that reveals people's unhappiness. Under the general hilarity, however, one feels that all six of Ayckbourn's characters are in some way strange or blighted. Norman himself is a shambling Fulham gigolo with an uncontrollable need to be loved but married to Ruth who is so full of the success ethic that she does not have any time left for people. Reg is stuck in a dream of perpetual, hobby-filled adolescence (he has one particularly wistful speech about boyhood happiness making balsa-wood aeroplanes) but eternally hitched to Sarah who treats life like a railway timetable. Annie is chained to a sick mother and waiting for some positive emotional commitment from Tom, the lugubrious vet who takes a good thirty seconds to decide whether or not he wants his coffee black or white.

What is even more significant is that Ayckbourn suggests that the three blood relations (Annie, Ruth and Reg) are all the victims of their oversexed, aberrant, bedridden, once bed-hopping mother. Ayckbourn is not, on the whole, a judgemental writer; but when he does point the finger at someone it is usually with good reason. In these three plays he never lets us forget the presence of the tyrannical old party upstairs. 'She's an evil old lady, that one', says Norman to Annie. 'No wonder you're all peculiar.' Rubbing the point in, Ayckbourn has her three progeny reminisce about her picking up a guy on the sands at Weston-super-Mare, being caught almost *in flagrante delicto* with a Polish rear-gunner and openly carrying on *affaires* under her husband's roof. Even now, she likes to have Annie read out the juicy bits from torrid romances and pretends that Tom is a human doctor so he can examine her in minute detail. Ayckbourn is always too shrewd to spell things out directly; but you sense that the mother's sexual voracity has driven Reg into his private bolt-hole, Ruth into the escape route of work and poor Annie into a lifetime of careworn subservience. Ayckbourn does not usually deal in villains; but, if *The Norman Conquests* has one, then it is definitely the harpie upstairs in the blue bed-jacket.

The hard thing to convey about the trilogy is just how funny it is. But there is nothing idle or empty about the laughter it induces. I remember that a month after *The Norman Conquests* opened in Greenwich I witnessed in London a translated French farce by Gaby Bruyere, *Birds of Paradise*, in which a post-Victorian widow erroneously purchased a Caribbean brothel instead of the advertised riding-school. It was painfully unfunny because it had no visible contact with truth. But the Ayckbourn trilogy constantly makes us laugh because we see fragments of our own experience pushed to the outer limits.

Take the dinner-party scene from *Table Manners*. Sarah wants the family to have a 'civilised' meal and live up to a Platonic ideal of After Eight bourgeois elegance. Yet what actually happens when the family gets round the dinner table? Endless, musical-chairs squabbles about who sits where. One guest seated on a preposterously low stool. Bickering about the respective merits of childless and fertile marriages. Husband insulting wife and being struck by a guest who thinks it's his girl friend who's been vilified. Ingredients that would be funny anywhere, you may say; but the reason we laugh so loudly here is that they happen to characters we have come to know and who are straining hard to conform to a notion of normal family life. The joke is that human desperation will keep breaking through.

Technically, *The Norman Conquests* shows Ayckbourn pushing his personal frontiers outwards (in one sense, he turns playwriting into a heightened game, intellectual self-entertainment). But the theme that binds the play together is the one that links all his plays from *Relatively Speaking* onwards: the notion that our social and domestic lives are full of strange rituals that no longer relate to our actual behaviour. Other dramatists might relate this to the Decline of the West, the Decay of Capitalism or the Collapse of the Bourgeois Ethic. Still others might propose some radical solution. But Ayckbourn is not a prescriptive or nakedly political writer. He offers no solutions. He does, however, recognise the problems. He is a very funny writer but a deeply serious one who turns behaviour into social comment. *The Norman Conquests* (the best comic trilogy in the theatre since Goldoni's *La Trilogia della villeggiatura* in 1761) certainly brings Ayckbourn's quest for truth-through-laughter to a certain kind of fulfilment. The question now was how far he could go in pushing pain to the forefront.

4
Laughing Till It Hurts

Before pursuing Ayckbourn's fascination with comic pain, it is worth taking a look at a little known television play, *Service Not Included*, that he wrote in 1974 for a BBC Television drama series called *Masquerade*. The play is not published and Ian Watson's *Conversations with Ayckbourn* makes clear it was a pretty wretched experience. Ayckbourn wrote it at the behest of a TV director friend, Herbert Wise. Having been told by the BBC with its usual flair for competence that he need not worry about cast requirements and sets, he found he had to cut down drastically on his original twenty-four characters and thirty-eight separate settings. 'Because of the technical complexities which I'd set, Herbie, on location – two days in a pub in Berkshire – was having his work cut out: some scenes he never got in can at all because he had no time. So it was OK, but it was very far from what it was intended originally to be – a waiter's-eye-view of a dreadful office party.'

Yet the script of *Service Not Included* is very interesting;

for it shows Ayckbourn, even when working the prescribed format of a series of half-hour telly plays about fancy-dress parties, returning to several of his familiar themes. Marital disappointment. The crass insensitivity of the managerial classes. Above all, the misery and deception that often bubble away beneath worn-out social rituals. He takes some telly executive's dumb idea for a series and invests it with something revealing and particular.

The framework is a company do in a mock-antique country-house hotel at the end of a four-day conference: a letting-your-hair-down occasion for middle management and their wives who cavort around the hotel in Tyrolean drag, frogman's flippers, mermaid's tails, Viking uniform or Spanish gypsy costume and who represent characters as various as Dracula and Florence Nightingale. We, however, in script form, view the action through the cynical eyes of Jace, a white-jacketed waiter who has seen office Bacchanalia come and go and who regards the action with the bleary detachment of a tourist guide watching Norwegians in anoraks ploughing through a stately home. What to the desk wallahs and their wives is a big night out is to the hotel staff merely one in a long line of alcoholic, adulterous, slightly desultory routs. This immediately gives Ayckbourn a fix on the duplicity and despair underneath the ritual hoop-la.

The action starts on the steps of the three-star hotel with Jace smoking a quiet, pre-function cigarette. The camera then tracks after him as he serves drinks to Donald, a pushy company man who has come to the party with a bulging dossier for reorganising the advertising account, which he is going to thrust on the boss despite the advice of his wife, Cathy; to Neil, a philandering subordinate, and his wife Freda who drowns her solitude in drink; to Warwick, the dinner-jacketed big white chief, accompanied by his wife and a pig-faced smoothie in Regency attire. The whole point is that Jace, as he moves between the Tudor Bar, the Foyers and the upstairs rooms, sees things other characters do not; that he alone understands the real nature of what is going on at a supposedly festive occasion with Nordic warriors doing congas through the hotel lobbies.

So it is Jace (along with us) who discovers, by delivering champers to room 304, that Neil is having an adulterous fling with Cathy, wife of the overachieving Donald. He also learns, as he delivers the drinks to Warwick's table, that Donald's plan for reorganising the advertising budget is received with stiff politeness; he is even given the job of dumping Donald's folder, when Warwick has seen him off, in the trash can behind the bar counter. As he makes periodic trips to the bar to collect orders, he sees Neil's wife getting steadily plastered, hears later that she has fallen off a stool and sees a bucket of water being provided to wash up the hotel steps whither she has repaired. Jace is at everyone's beck and call. But he is a witness to their adultery, their drunkenness, their lies (as Donald pretends he has put in a word for Neil with the boss) and also to the brutal indifference of top management as they discard the employees' suggestions they have solicited in the company magazine. At the end Jace prepares to go home, taking out of his top pocket the dog-end he had lit at the beginning of the play:

HALL PORTER: No excitements, then?
JACE: When?
HALL PORTER: This evening.
JACE: Not so's you'd notice, no. 'Night.
HALL PORTER: Night.

And, as Jace makes his way out through the foyer doors, we realise this is par for the course in this kind of middle-class ritual.

Ayckbourn may have been disappointed with the way the play turned out: indeed felt a palpable sense of impotence as he sat in the control van watching it being recorded by a bloke more interested in catching the budget on ITV. However, it tells us several things. One is Ayckbourn's instant grasp of know-how: even when working in an alien medium he still manages to exploit the tricks of that particular trade. Instead of doing the obvious thing – such as swiftly intercutting between, say, a couple making love upstairs and the conniving and office-politicking going on several floors below – he gives us a waiter's-eye-view of events. Another is his ability to get instant visual comedy out of the contrast between the flamboyant costumes and the desperately unheroic lives actually being led: Neil's Dracula outfit makes the additional point that he is both a bloodsucking parasite and a sexual raver. Ayckbourn also lightly sketches in the class and power divisions: just as Warwick, the company director, keeps out of fancy dress and casually dumps staff submissions, so the Hotel Assistant Manager harries Jace and then retires to the privacy of his office to put his feet up and watch the box. Within the half-hour framework it is obviously not possible to explore characters in scorching depth. Yet, even here, Ayckbourn manages to show us that he is more than a cunning craftsman: even in a formula series, he manages to remind us that our social festivities are often a cover for a good deal of pain and dishonesty. In short, a masquerade.

Alan Ayckbourn

'Absent Friends'

This, of course, raises a key question about Ayckbourn. Is he always the same? Is he forever mining a particular, highly profitable seam of middle-class angst? Is there, in fact, any real development in his work?

My answer would be that any first-rate dramatist stakes out his own particular territory and lays proprietorial claim to it. Harold Pinter early on established himself as a master of comic menace fascinated by the power battles conducted within four walls. Peter Shaffer in almost everything he has written has been obsessed by the conflict within man between a toiling, desiccated rationalism and an instinctual, semi-divine fire and energy. Peter Nichols repeatedly uses popular forms, like vaudeville, pantomime and the musical, to give us fragments of painful autobiography. John Osborne is hooked on the notion of a truculent, combative, ferocious male ego seeking some answering chord in the people or society around him. Edward Bond constantly seeks a metaphor for the destructive violence that, from the very start of life, seems to cripple and squash human potential.

I do not deny that there are endless variations played on chosen themes; or that dramatists can, if they wish, suddenly break the mould. Pinter's *A Kind of Alaska*, for instance, is a realistic, moving account of a woman aroused from twenty-nine years of sleeping-sickness. Shaffer's *Black Comedy* is a hilarious farce about the convulsive gropings of people stumbling around a darkened room which is, on stage, blazingly lit. Tom Stoppard, after years of living with the accusation that he was mainly a pyrotechnic wordsmith, suddenly gave us a moving play about middle-class adultery in *The Real Thing*. Yet I still believe that the journalistic quest for novelty, for the leopard which violently changes his spots, is a hangover from the Romantic notion of the writer as a fluctuating, spontaneous, radically changing egocentric. The truth is that most writers, dramatists certainly, harbour prejudices, preoccupations, areas of life that they make particularly their own: what is important is how dexterously they manage to find new ways of expressing their abiding concerns.

By that token, Ayckbourn is a constant developer. His concerns may remain pretty constant. But his work gets darker in tone with time; and he is always experimenting with new forms. Technically, he is the most questing dramatist we possess in Britain today. All of which is borne out by his next play, *Absent Friends*, which followed a now familiar pattern by being premiered at Scarborough in June 1974 and being seen at the Garrick Theatre, London, in July 1975.

Here the experiment actually lies in discarding technical high-jinks for ruthless simplicity. Ayckbourn gives us a relatively straightforward situation – a consolatory tea party thrown for Colin by his former friends after the death by drowning of his fiancée – and then develops it with implacable dramatic logic. Stage time matches real time. The action is confined to a single set. The serious issues (including our tongue-tied, embarrassed modern response to death and the havoc-wreaking quality of idealists) are handled without a wealth of comic camouflage. Ayckbourn here proves emphatically he can handle pain. And the play has the bracing quality of a chaser after a month of Margueritas.

A novice would do well to ponder Ayckbourn's skilful, copybook dramaturgy: in particular, the way he creates a mood of nervous domestic tension even before Colin enters two-thirds of the way through the first act. The setting is a Saturday-afternoon tea party in an open-plan living room. The hosts are Paul and Diana.

Paul is a monstrously egoistic executive (a type Ayckbourn always treats with fascinated repulsion) who rises early, works late, plays a mean game of squash and has sundry *affaires*: a suburban Lothario with a black briefcase. Diana is aware that she lacks his dynamism but is convinced that she provides the emotional security he needs. She is pretty certain, however, that he is having an *affaire* with one of her teatime guests, Evelyn, a morose gum-chewer who works as a cashier at the Rollarena, is constantly immersed in women's magazines as if they were a pulp drug and makes little attempt to communicate with her husband, John, her baby or anyone else. As for John, he is a restless, change-jingling, incompetent, third-rate salesman who accepts his wife's brief, abortive fling with Paul because the latter is his one hope of economic survival. (All big fleas, in Ayckbourn, have little fleas upon their back to bite them.) Which leaves Marge, a childless fusspot, who babytalks to her absent husband, Gordon, an incipient cricketer who is now a Fire Prevention Officer living in a semi-permanent state of bedbound illness. By the first of several ironies, these are the broken reeds gathered to offer comfort to the supposedly disconsolate Colin.

The next thing I would point out to a novice is the way Ayckbourn not merely signals the storm clouds ahead but does it in a different way for each person. Thus Diana suggests that she is on the edge of a half-marital, half-menopausal breakdown by the way she indulges in a compulsive monologue to Evelyn about her own inadequacy and her husband's infidelity. It is partly a device to smoke Evelyn from her adulterous lair. It is partly a demonstration of neurosis. It is also creepily funny:

DIANA: . . . But I will not stand deception. I'm simply asking that I be told. Either by him or if not by her. Not necessarily now but sometime. You see.
(*A pause. Evelyn is expressionless.*)
I know he is, you see. He's not very clever and he's a very bad liar like most men. If he takes the trouble, like last Saturday, to tell me he's just going down the road to the football match he might at least choose a Saturday when they're playing at home.

Just as Diana's relentless volubility is a sign of her insecurity, so Evelyn's totally expressionless, gum-chewing taciturnity is a sign of her blank misery and numbed withdrawal. She brings to mind Pam in Edward Bond's *Saved* in the way she rocks her baby's pram with mechanical listlessness, takes no evident interest in what is said to her and is only roused from her catatonic passivity when Marge asks her point-blank if she and Paul are having an *affair*. She announces that they once made love in the back of Paul's car whereupon she told him: 'That was about as exciting as being made love to by a sack of clammy cement and would he kindly drive me home'. Meanwhile Marge, the third of this doomed trinity, has the relentless busyness of the childless married woman for whom the husband becomes a substitute kid: in her ceaseless telephone calls to the bedridden Gordon (whom she addresses as Jumjums) you feel she has positively mothered him into illness.

Susan Fleetwood once remarked to me that Ayckbourn is one of the few modern writers who offers decent parts for actresses. But it is not simply a matter of juicy roles: I feel he has a marked compassion for women. His plays are all about blighted lives. But whereas you feel he has little patience with thrusting, bustling males, he constantly sees

married women, in particular, as people whose lives have
been irreversibly damaged through little fault of their
own. He is not condescending or patronising towards them
as a sex. He merely endorses Joyce Cary's observation that
every woman's life is, in some sense, a tragedy.

Indeed, in setting the scene before Colin's arrival,
Ayckbourn is decidedly less charitable towards the men.
Paul is clearly a gold-plated monster who addresses the
women in real Naked Ape terms ('Mother's meeting, is
it?'), takes a cursory look at Evelyn's baby ('What's in
there, tomorrow's dinner?'), pretends he did not know
Colin was coming, retreats behind a barrier of work and is
unfeelingly lecherous ('He's halfway through the Yellow
Pages by now', says Evelyn. 'If it moves, he's on to it').
Upwardly mobile men on the make (like Sidney Hopcroft)
are favourite Ayckbourn targets: men who have actually
made it and squandered their humanity in the process are
people he deeply despises. He is more tolerant towards
John, the restless jigger and change-jingler, the snapper-up
of cheap, useless bargains, the complaisant cuckold,
because at least with him, cheerfulness keeps breaking in.

But what is impressive theatrically is the way Ayckbourn
builds up an atmosphere of orchestrated chaos. A tea party
is meant to be a ritual of decorum and politeness; but
before it has got under way and the principal guest has
arrived, we have Diana openly accusing Paul of infidelity,
Evelyn trying to leave in a huff with her crying baby,
Marge on the phone to a desperate Gordon who has spilt
cough mixture on his sheet. All these things are happening
as Colin is ringing the doorbell trying to get in. All reveal
Ayckbourn's familiar ability not merely to *tell* you things
but to *show* you their consequences. We know from the
start that Diana is on the edge of hysteria. But to have her
erupting seconds before Colin's arrival is both to

demonstrate the precariousness of our social rituals and to prepare the way for Colin's advance into a domestic minefield. These people have turned out on a Saturday to give succour and comfort to the bereaved: but the truth is that they really cannot stand each other.

That is the key irony: I would also point out to a beginner playwright the way Ayckbourn compounds it with another irony. He has Colin turn out to be not the heartbroken reed we had all been expecting but an infallibly cheerful fellow ever-ready to talk about his drowned fiancée and even more ready, with stunning inaccuracy, to put his finger on what is wrong with everyone else's lives. He is a smiling, suburban Gregers Werle. But his presence also raises the central problem which is that no-one knows any more how to cope with death. To us, death is the Great Unmentionable; or, when it is mentioned, something to be swathed in cosmetic euphemisms. Ayckbourn hits hard, showing how our petty social rituals are limpingly inadequate to cope with the fact that we all die:

DIANA: . . . I think I can speak for all of us, Colin, when I say how very sorry we are to hear about your loss. As I hope you'll realise, we're your friends and – well – and although we didn't know Carol – none of us had the pleasure of meeting her – we feel that in a small way, your grief is our grief. After all, in this world, we are all to some extent – we're all – what's the word. . . .?

PAUL: Joined.

DIANA: No.

JOHN: Related.

MARGE: Combined.

DIANA: No. Dependent.

PAUL: That's what I said.

DIANA: No you didn't, you said joined or something.

PAUL: It's the same thing. Joined, dependent, means the same.

DIANA: We are all dependent in a way for our own – and well . . . no, I'm sorry I've forgotten what I was going to say now. I hope you understand what I meant anyway.

COLIN: Thank you.

DIANA: Oh well, that's got that over with anyway. I mean – more tea, anyone?

That, to me, is vintage Ayckbourn. He is making both a specific dramatic point and a more general, social one: that these so-called friends turn even a tribute to death into fractious quarrelling and that, in our age, we are embarrassed to say simply 'we are members one of another'. We preserve the hollow rituals of togetherness. But our language, our feelings, our sensitivities are so stunted that we cannot clearly express our sense of human belonging. Only Colin in this particular group speaks his mind without restraint: the trouble is that he suffers the moral myopia of the truly happy and fails to see the hornet's nest he is stirring up. Indeed when he launches into a long eulogy about the dead Carol, he drives Diana into hysterical tears, John into physical queasiness, Marge into lachrymose snorting and the others into a panic-stricken silence.

In the second act, the few remaining protective layers are stripped away and truths laid bare. That is a familiar enough dramatic process. Albee in *Who's Afraid of Virginia Woolf* does it through tongue-loosening alcohol. Priestley in *Dangerous Corner* does it through a reverberative chance remark. Ibsen in *The Wild Duck* does it through misplaced missionary idealism. All these plays are subconscious ancestors of *Absent Friends*. But Ayckbourn triggers off disaster through a well-meaning, bereaved friend who assiduously rakes over everyone's past. Colin's motives are the kindest possible. The effects are calamitous.

It is part of Ayckbourn's craft that Colin not only gets everyone wrong: he also precipitates dramatic crisis with Cheeryble-like bonhomie. Thus he blithely reminisces about the one-time passion that Paul (with whom he went a-wooing) entertained for Diana and she for him. He recalls how she used to talk for hours over cups of coffee about Paul. On another occasion, Paul picked up a napkin of hers, secreted it in his pocket and took it home to act as a reminder of her presence. The romantic mood Colin laboriously recreates is, however, quickly shattered:

PAUL: You know something, Col.

COLIN: What?

PAUL: I've just remembered. I've still got that table napkin of hers, you know.

COLIN: Have you really?

PAUL: Yes. I use it to clean the car with.

(*Diana picks up the cream jug and pours it slowly over Paul's head. Paul sits for a moment stunned.*)

The audience rejoices: Paul had it coming. What is striking is Ayckbourn's peppering of two types of male insensitivity. On the one hand, there is the piggish coarseness of Paul who not only knows that his love for Diana has gone sour but feels obliged to advertise the fact to everyone in the room. But there is also the equally culpable thickness of Colin who is myopically unaware of the havoc he is creating. The wretched Diana is driven to nervous breakdown and blush-making, rambling confessions about a teenage urge to join the Royal Canadian Mounted Police. John is propelled to confess that: 'In fact, apart from me, we are the most miserable family you are ever likely to meet and I'm working on me'. The mothering Marge has a row over the telephone – interrupted, needless to say, by Colin on the extension – with Gordon whose hot-water bottle has burst. Hitherto precarious relationships are left in pieces, thanks to the tenacious goodness and irresistible urge to reminisce of the terrifying Colin.

Absent Friends is a fine play because it maximises the central irony: the sentimental man who brings disaster in his wake. Like all good plays, it is also rooted in a plausible past: a past in which Paul was once an avid wooer rather than a cynical roué, in which Gordon was a promising left-arm fast bowler rather than a physical wreck, in which John was a live wire instead of a restless parasite. Colin himself (memorably incarnated in the West End by Richard Briers with mouth permanently agape like a hungry sea-lion and fist constantly jabbing people in proof of rapidly vanishing fellow-feeling) is so well observed that you can envisage the emotional mayhem wherever he goes. He tells us, for example, about Carol's parents: 'I'm always round with them these days. You know, talking over old times and things. And if I get a bit depressed, out come the old albums'. Suddenly you get a nightmarish, snapshot image of a weeping mother and a distraught father as Colin sits on the sofa serenely smiling at pictures of his late fiancée and thinking he is making everyone happy.

Alan Brien, though questioning the up-market setting and the age gaps between the actors in the London production, got it right in *Plays and Players* when he said:

'*Absent Friends* is a serious, almost clinical, presentation of the serious nature of marriage where the most painful moments occur, not when the participants recognise its weaknesses, but when the outsider mistakes them for strengths'. The gap between what we are and what other people perceive us to be is at the core of this intimate, low-key, funny-painful play. You've heard of light comedy? This is light tragedy showing Ayckbourn digging deeper than ever before into marital misery (Diana's breakdown is real) and outsiderish incomprehension. Ayckbourn has also preserved in aspic a classic character: the cheerful wrecker. And, although the play is anchored in a comfortable, bourgeois modern world, one can see it making sense to an audience 50 or 100 years hence. As long as there are people who carry disaster about with them, in the way others carry some rare disease, and all the time think they are doing good, the play will still be relevant. Simple in form, it is powerful in effect. Through nervous, edgy laughter, it shows Ayckbourn suggesting that the best friends are indeed those who are usually absent.

'Confusions'

1974 was one of Ayckbourn's busiest years. *The Norman Conquests* and *Absurd Person Singular* were running concurrently in the West End. The latter opened at the Music Box on Broadway. *Absent Friends* made its bow in Scarborough in June. And *Confusions*, five interlinked one-act plays, had its Scarborough premiere in September (it did not reach the Apollo Theatre, London, until May 1976). Around this time I also suggested in a piece in the *Guardian* that Ayckbourn was a left-wing writer using a right-wing form: within the format of farcical comedy, I claimed, he was saying some fairly atrabilious things about the breakdown of middle-class manners and the interaction of sex and class in English life. I stand by the point even if I would, on reflection, slightly modify the terms. To me, Ayckbourn has always been a deeply deceptive writer. His plays have an iron-clad sense of form, almost invariably provoke laughter and are swallowed up by the traditional theatregoing audience. Yet they are anything but cosy. They seduce audiences with the promise of sweets. Yet they slip them the bitter pill of recognition and increasingly leave them in a state of prickly discomfort. Ayckbourn gives theatregoers a good night out. But he also leaves them asking themselves, 'Are we really like that?'

I would say this applies even to a relatively minor work like *Confusions*. It was popular without ever quite achieving the mythic success of other Ayckbourn plays: perhaps because of a built-in English resistance to one-acters. Its five pieces also range in tone from the broadly farcical to the quietly comic, yet in all of them is a persistent fascination with solitaries stuck in some obsessional groove. Julian Jebb was on the ball when he said that the title was one of the few things wrong with this collection of plays. 'They're concerned', he suggested, 'more with separation, obsession and isolation; but these are words we would expect to find on the covers of Pelican sociology books rather than on a Shaftesbury Avenue marquee'.

What the plays send my mind back to is Henri Bergson's classic book on *Laughter*. Theorising about the comic is always a dangerous business but Bergson's book is full of wisdom and sanity. He starts with three basic assumptions. That the comic does not exist outside the pale of what is human: in other words, that a landscape, a hat, an animal are never inherently laughable. That there is a certain absence of feeling which usually accompanies laughter. And that the intelligence which responds to the comic must remain in touch with other intelligences: 'however spontaneous it seems, laughter always implies a kind of secret freemasonry, or even complicity, with other laughers, real or imaginary'.

He pursues his theory in detail, suggesting that 'any arrangement of acts and events is comic which gives us, in a single combination, the illusion of life and the distinct impression of a mechanical arrangement'. In other words, a realistic situation is combined with a certain human inflexibility. A human being may become like a jack-in-the-box with a repressed feeling going off again and again like a spring. And Bergson takes as an example a scene from Molière's *Tartuffe* in which the maid tries to tell the duped and hypnotised Orgon about his wife's illness while the latter interrupts with enquiries as to the health of Tartuffe ('Et Tartuffe?') repeated every few moments to give the sensation of a spring being released. Orgon is here behaving like a machine in a credible human situation. Indeed the bedrock of Bergson's theories is that: 'We laugh every time a person gives us the impression of being a thing'. This may take the form of Sancho Panza being tossed in the air like a football; of two men beating each other with sticks till they resemble solid wooden dummies; or of Molière's Scapin manipulating other characters so that they lose their freedom and become like dancing-jacks.

My contention is that Bergson's theory is borne out by the five plays in *Confusions*. In the first piece, *Mother Figure*, we see a woman, Lucy, who is so lonely, so childridden, so entrapped by the demands of motherhood that she treats her adult neighbours precisely as if they were kids. The two neighbours simply come round to deliver a phone message from Lucy's husband: they are offered orange juice and milk to drink, instructed not to eat all the choccy bics and, when one of them stomps angrily out and his wife starts to cry, Lucy brandishes a particularly nasty-looking toy in her face saying, 'Mr Poddle's watching you. You don't want Mr Poddle to see you crying, do you?' In Bergsonian terms, we laugh because: 'Any individual is comic who automatically goes his own way without troubling himself about getting into touch with the rest of his fellow-beings'. So we laugh at Lucy because she is incapable any longer of distinguishing between a child and an adult. The only point where Bergson's theory does not apply to Ayckbourn is in its idea of correction. 'It is part of laughter', says Bergson, 'to reprove the individual's absent-mindedness and wake him out of his dream.' But the pathos of Ayckbourn's Lucy is that she seems to be permanently trapped inside her maternal mask.

Mother Figure occupies no more than fifteen minutes of stage time. But its idea of human rigidity and pathetic isolation is carried over into the next play, *Drinking Companion*, where we see Lucy's travelling, *haute-couture* salesman husband, Harry, desperately trying to chat up a woodenly unseduceable perfume saleslady in the bar of a provincial hotel. It is a common enough situation: indeed the waiter has something of the sniffy, seen-it-all before quality of the hero of *Service Not Included*. But what lifts the play out of the rut is Harry's intoxicated, unbudgeable persistence. Like his wife, with whom apparently he lives on only the most formal terms, he is so locked into his solitude that he cannot see the effect he is having: even though the object of his affections is about as penetrable as Fort Knox he persists in throwing his room key on to the table in the hope she will pick it up. I am not, of course, suggesting that Ayckbourn sat down to demonstrate Bergson's theories. But his own growing fascination with the texture of ordinary despair and the blocking-up of normal feelings (strongly present in *Absurd Person Singular* and *Absent Friends*) leads him towards a study of people-as-automata.

Sometimes, of course, this automaton-like behaviour springs from professional function. Bergson sees this too when he talks about the individual who performs his duty like a machine. He tells the story of a large steamer wrecked off the coast of Dieppe. The passengers, wet, tired and exhausted, were rescued with great difficulty. As they were brought, shivering and flaked-out to the shore, a customs officer rushed to their assistance crying 'Have you anything to declare?'

Something similar happens in the third piece in this quintet, *Between Mouthfuls*, which is about two vehemently quarrelling couples in a restaurant being served by a waiter who maintains a smiling, inflexible courtesy even as their lives fall apart. This being Ayckbourn, he builds on the joke by giving us only the fragments of conversation that the waiter himself overhears; and by linking the couples so that the wife at one table is revealed to have had an *affaire* with her husband's boss who is sitting at the other. But the real humdinger is the way the waiter smoothly and insinuatingly doles out the lobster, the chicken, the salad, the vegetables and the wine even as a couple of marriages crack under his very nose. John Alderton played the waiter in the West End with a wonderful laconic authority as he went about his business:

WAITER: Vegetables, sir?
MARTIN: Er – just carrots. Rome? What were you doing in Rome?

POLLY: I was with Donald Pearce.

MARTIN: Donald Pearce – that's fine, thank you – what were you doing with Donald Pearce?

POLLY: I spent three weeks with Donald Pearce in a hotel in Rome.

MARTIN: My God. (*He puts his head in his hands on the table.*)

WAITER: Potatoes, sir?

It is a sign of Ayckbourn's mastery of situation that those two simple words – 'Potatoes, sir?' – produced one of the biggest laughs of the evening; but then nearly every comic dramatist will confirm that laughs often come from a well-planned 'Yes' or 'No' rather than some laboriously polished epigram.

But Ayckbourn carried the joke about mechanical obsessiveness to the outer limits of lunacy in the fourth play, *Gosforth's Fête*, the memory of which even now produces paroxysms of mirth. Someone (not Bergson) said that farce was a matter of rearranging the furniture on the Titanic. And that is what happens in this pocket miracle in which a village publican desperately tries to keep festivities going at a fête as news of his having impregnated a local lass is broadcast over the public address system, as the girl's scoutmaster boy friend goes drunkenly berserk, as an unquenchable tea urn pours hot liquid everywhere, as a Tory Councillor's wife gets electrocuted while making the opening speech and as a scaffolding collapses under the weight of a group of semi-delinquent Wolf Cubs. The idea of a hideously awful fête in which everything goes awry is as old as the hills. Yet who, before Ayckbourn, had put it on stage? What is more he does it with a genuine feeling for the realities of village life (everyone, it turns out, knew about the village maiden's impregnation except the hapless dad and the baggy-trousered cubmaster) and with a wonderful appetite for mounting disaster. This is what Bergson calls 'the snow-ball effect' where everything grows by arithmetical progression. But what counts on stage is the sheer visual invention: never shall I forget the spectacle of scalding tea pouring out of an urn while people run round with a relay race of cups in an effort to staunch its Niagara-like flow. Such is the power of the image that it becomes a reference point in real life: I recently saw in a BBC corridor a newly installed automatic-vending machine going bananas and dispensing endless cups of steaming hot chocolate while a frantic producer tried to cope with the merciless fluid. People turned to each other at the time and muttered 'Pure Ayckbourn'.

Only in the fifth play, *A Talk in the Park*, does Ayckbourn bang home too hard his general point that we are all victims of some rigid, ungovernable obsession: what we get here is a round of monologues with a sequence of solitary beings on park benches offloading their problems on to the next person while ignoring the plight of the person they have just come from. In defining mechanical behaviour, it too becomes mechanical: once you have got the general pattern, you can see the next move coming a mile off.

But the mild tedium of this last piece does nothing to lessen the impact of a series of plays that vividly demonstrate Ayckbourn's ability to transmute pain into comedy, to deal with all the fashionable themes of loneliness, non-communication and self-absorption while giving us some cracking laughs. He does it by building on a foundation of truthful characters; pushing those characters as far as they will go in a given situation; and building into the situation a series of visual gags as firmly embedded as cement in brickwork. Julian Jebb, writing about the Apollo production, said very significantly: 'The theatrical invention of the director and writer becomes indivisible from character itself'. That is it in a nutshell: Ayckbourn is serious and funny at the same time because the people are true.

'Jeeves'

And then came *Jeeves*: Ayckbourn's first brush with real West End disaster and a show that gave rise in many critics to what John Updike calls 'the delicate stink of affront'. It opened at Her Majesty's in April 1975 to fairly crucifying reviews (my own included) and closed just over a month later. How could it happen to a show that seemed to have all the ingredients of success – at its source the Jeeves stories of P. G. Wodehouse, book and lyrics by Ayckbourn, music by the *wunderkind* of *Jesus Christ Superstar*, Andrew Lloyd Webber?

Ayckbourn himself gave a large part of the answer when bluntly asked by Michael Coveney in an interview – Why was *Jeeves* so disastrous?

I was originally asked by Tim Rice and Andrew Lloyd Webber to prepare a book, which I did. When I turned up with the synopsis, Rice, I discovered, had decided that he couldn't cope with the lyrics, so I got conned into doing them. Already the thing was becoming a bigger commitment than I had originally envisaged. I don't think I could ever collaborate with another writer, but I did find collaborating with a musician very stimulating. The book, however, was eventually running for four hours. I could have cut it in about a day in Scarborough circumstances. But with a vehicle like that, by the time one gets round to cutting, it was like treading on eggs. Actors all had their numbers, the musicians had their favourite bits and so on. The producer of *Jeeves* I met twice as he spent most of his time in Los Angeles. We were all left to our own devices, which would have been all right if any of us had done this sort of show before. We badly needed Hal Prince, or someone like him. I did, however, develop a close working relationship with Lloyd Webber, which I hope might lead to something else, something conducted on our own terms. I was very impressed by *Company* which although a bit Manhattanish for English audiences, was undoubtedly something of a breakthrough. I'd like very much to try and write a commuter-belt musical with an original book.

This candid account of why *Jeeves* went wrong was confirmed when I took part in a television discussion with its director, the late and much admired Eric Thompson. Asked by Bryan Magee if the critics had killed the show, he said simply: 'No. The show killed the show'. Rarely have I heard such an honest admission. But, examining more closely why *Jeeves* produced such critical venom and died so quickly, I suspect it had a lot to do with the discrepancy between the quality of the enterprise and the scale of the production. It was really a small-scale story about Bertie Wooster's involvement with a trio of girls and about the puncturing of the high-stepping Fascist ambitions of Sir Roderick Spode. But it got blown up into another Big British Musical, an expensive event staged in the daunting rococo arena of Her Majesty's Theatre.

Listen dispassionately now to Lloyd Webber's tunes and Ayckbourn's lyrics and you find charm, guile and fey grace. There is still too much Bertie (David Hemmings had thirteen numbers to put across in the final version), too little Jeeves; and there is still excessive reliance on a pastel-coloured gentility. But Ayckbourn, though no Sondheim, writes lyrics that are often delicately pungent. The best of the numbers, 'Female of the Species', is a mini-madrigal about omnivorous womanhood boasting lines like:

Mother Nature has discovered women should be made to love,
Dainty daughter – skin like velvet – but there's steel inside the glove.

and:

When a woman takes a lover, finds a man whom she adores,
Those who cross her soon discover, little girls have razor claws.

In the delightful 'Eulalie' (the number that puts the finger on the British Fascist, Sir Roderick Spode) Ayckbourn also plays around lyrically with the last two syllables in a doodling, dotty Helen Morganish style. And there is a lazy Buchananesque charm to Bertie's declaration of principles in which he enquires: 'What can a chap do without it, How would he get through without it, The Code of the Woosters?'

What happened to *Jeeves*, I am convinced with the luxury of hindsight, was what happens to so many musicals: content was overlaid with style. A light, lyrical musical of the kind Wodehouse himself often penned for New York's jewel-like Princess Theatre was killed by the deadly hand of showbiz. We need in fact to do for musicals what we regularly do for classic plays, which is to discover the hidden work inside the spectacle by staging them in studio or intimate-rep conditions. The whole Sondheim canon could be profitably re-evaluated if we could see the works staged in small spaces (Sondheim without the Prince, in fact) where we could fasten on to the lyric sharpness. Some of the myriad sunken wrecks of the British musical might turn out to be not so disastrous after all if we could scrap the trappings and get to the core.

Meanwhile although *Jeeves* answered the question about Ayckbourn that George Axelrod had once asked of Neil Simon ('Has he got a flop in him?'), it did not in the end do his career any lasting damage: indeed it may have done him some good in that it nudged him in the direction of the chamber musical which he has explored in Scarborough over the last few years with the help of Paul Todd. Precisely because *Jeeves* was so rhetorically and extravagantly condemned (*mea culpa*), it bred an admiring counter-reaction. Ronald Bryden spoke for a defensive minority (including Harold Hobson and Irving Wardle) when he wrote in *Plays and Players*:

Most of what is right about *Jeeves* is Alan Ayckbourn's book, the most literate and genuinely witty a British musical comedy has offered since Sandy Wilson's *Valmouth*. Ayckbourn has grasped the essence of Wodehouse's comedy: the way his swift, curlicued dramatic monologues, strewn with fractured quotation and embroidered cliché, counterpoint and sophisticate the old-fashioned farce plots and characters he borrowed from 1920s musical comedy. Wodehouse himself called his novels musical comedies without music, and several in fact were re-workings of shows he wrote with Guy Bolton during their long partnership as Broadway's most successful book-and-lyrics team. His style was the written equivalent of first-rate comic acting, bringing to his naïve plot materials the vitality, intelligence and complicity with his audience over the head, so to speak, of the story which a star comedian brings to a role. So Ayckbourn wisely makes *Jeeves* a musical comedy narrated by Bertie Wooster, in one of his misguided attempts at village-hall entertainment, with occasional assistance and correction from his peerless valet, mentor and Machiavel of the title.

Perhaps *Jeeves* was less of an utter catastrophe than a diversion from Ayckbourn's self-appointed task of stripping the protective, onion-like layers off middle-class life. It says much for his constant resilience as a writer that two months after he had been implicated in a major theatrical flop, he had a new comedy ready for the Library Theatre, Scarborough, and one that was to become one of the biggest money-spinners of them all – Ayckbourn was simply unputdownable.

'Bedroom Farce'

In *Absent Friends* and *Confusions* Ayckbourn showed that he was much more than what John Osborne somewhat dismissively called 'a right-wing boulevardier'. That he could handle such themes as empty social rituals, destructive niceness, fenced-off personal solitude, the sheer awfulness of so much middle-class life without losing his comic perspective. So it is a slight surprise to find him coming up next with a robust laughter-maker like *Bedroom Farce* (which opened in Scarborough in June 1975 and which was produced by the National Theatre in London in March 1977). Even Ayckbourn himself, when he talked to Ian Watson, sounded faintly amazed that his subconscious had propelled him towards a comic riot:

> I felt rather extraordinary when I wrote it, though: I didn't quite know why I'd written it. It was very strange. It cropped up in the middle of my serious phase: this rather jolly play suddenly arrived. And I think I was rather rude to it. I said to it 'I'm an *Absent Friends* man now, a much more serious dramatist'. I always liked *Absent Friends* but that's just blatant prejudice for a play that's had fewer productions than any other.

My own feeling is that *Bedroom Farce* (one of his very best) is actually just as 'serious' as Ayckbourn's doomier plays. It carries an audience along on an almost unending crest of laughter; but that laughter is anything but mindless. For what is the play actually about? What Schopenhauer called 'the tyranny of the weak', the capacity of a neurotic married couple not only to export their problems but also to exacerbate the crises in other people's marriages. It also deals with parental destructiveness, marital violence, failures of communication, male vanity. Where a lesser dramatist might set up these themes and then find an action that illustrated them, Ayckbourn sets up a brilliantly comic device, lets his imagination take over and allows the ideas to spring out of exact observation of human behaviour. He reminds us all the time that a play is an artefact, a toy, a construct; but that, at its best, it can also illuminate the human condition.

Bedroom Farce is also one of those rare plays in which form and content achieve a blissfully happy marriage (about the only one on view). Ayckbourn presents us with three bedrooms occupied at various stages of the evening by four couples (Trevor and Susannah are the wild cards floating either singly or jointly from one bedroom to another). Bedrooms have featured in plenty of plays before but they are normally associated with illicit sex and are places to which people repair rather than settings for revelations of character (Jan de Hartog's marital comedy, *The Fourposter*, is the only exception I can think of). So the notion of three bedrooms on view simultaneously is both a nice comic sight-gag (and it's a measure of the idea's theatricality that the Granada TV production failed because it had to cut from one bedroom to the other rather than keeping them all in focus) and a wonderful chance to explore the recesses of private behaviour, the bits of ourselves we show to our sleeping partners rather than the world at large.

By having three bedrooms and four couples, Ayckbourn also finds the perfect visual metaphor for his theme: that the utterly self-absorbed hawk their neuroses around like door-to-door salesmen inflicting damage wherever they go. Trevor and Susannah are the odd couple out who carry their child-like marital squabbles around from place to place. In the first act they arrive explosively at a party being thrown by a larky, joshing, practical-joking couple of young marrieds, Malcolm and Kate, and not only proceed to wreck it but to drive a wedge between host and hostess. In the second act, Susannah repairs to her in-laws, Delia and Ernest, and not only ruins their decorous midnight feast but also exposes their generational failure to communicate. Meanwhile Trevor winds up with Jan, an old flame, and her bed-bound husband Nick who seem to exist in a state of easily fractured mutual tolerance. Like earlier Ayckbourn protagonists, Trevor and Susannah are agents of chaos. But they are also something more:

unwrappers of the frail tissue paper that surrounds other people's marriages.

Take Ernest and Delia. They are Trevor's parents, occupy a large Victorian bedroom and are swathed in a contented twilit pathos. 'You can tell a great deal from people's bedrooms', says Delia and we learn a lot from theirs. Their antiquated period furniture is matched by slightly antiquated moral attitudes and a feeling that they have never quite made it into the modern world. In one of Ayckbourn's funniest scenes, they return from an anniversary dinner at a poshly awful restaurant and make up for their hunger by eating pilchards on toast while Ernest reads chapters from his favourite book, *Tom Brown's Schooldays*. The choice of book is no accident: it suggests that Ernest is one of those charming, bumbling, emotionally arrested, elderly English public-schoolboys whose language ('Good show') and outlook have never progressed much beyond the Reform. And it is wonderfully typical that Delia after all these years still cannot plug into the Thomas Hughes classic, uttering the memorable cry, in the midst of Ernest's reading, of 'Who are all these people?'

It is only with the eruption of the demented Susannah, trailing her exposed nerve ends, that we really begin to glimpse the chasm of non-communication that exists between Delia and Ernest. Incensed that she has found Trevor in the act of kissing his old girl friend, Jan, and claiming that she herself is despised by him, Susannah passionately asks: 'Do you know what it's like to be ignored?' To which, Delia replies, 'Well, yes. As a matter of fact, I do'. As delivered by Joan Hickson at the National Theatre, those lines evoked a whole lifetime of emotional solitude. And when Susannah goes on to suggest that she is talking about sexual as well as mental solitude,

Delia (who always refers to words like B-E-D and S-E-X in permanent capital letters) confesses that she would rather talk to her doctor than her husband about physical matters. Susannah does not merely ruin everyone's sleep by driving Ernest into a dampened spare room where the steam rises off his blanket, by having incandescent nightmares and by making dawn phone calls. She herself shows that the obsessively confessional modern marriage is some kind of reaction against the very English notion of a couple spending half a lifetime side by side in a state of semi-detachment.

Ayckbourn makes Delia and Ernest funny-pathetic (rather like the supposedly murderous parents in *Family Circles*). But although he sees the comedy in these co-habiting strangers, he does not let them entirely off the hook. One of his running themes (there again in *The Norman Conquests*) is that we are most of us the maimed, damaged victims of heredity; and, if Trevor is one of life's emotional walking wounded, it is pretty clear who is responsible:

DELIA: He was always a difficult boy. I sometimes think if you hadn't ignored him quite as much –

ERNEST: I did?

DELIA: Of course you did. You hardly said a word to him all the time he was growing up.

ERNEST: I seem to remember chatting away to him for hours.

DELIA: Well. Chatting. I meant conversation. Conversation about important things. A father should converse with his son. About things that matter deeply.

ERNEST: Doesn't really leave much to talk about then, does it?

It is amazing that in the course of a rollicking comedy Ayckbourn pins down so much of the emotional shyness of middle-class England.

If Delia and Ernest embody antique isolation, Malcolm and Kate in their terraced-house front bedroom represent animal exuberance. They are youngish, fond of practical jokes (spraying each other with shaving-cream, hiding shoes in pillows and hairbrushes in bed) and slightly self-conscious about their normality. Susannah's revelation that she is attracted by passing girls in the street leads to a wonderful bit of Malcolm–Kate bedroom talk in which we learn that he has girlie magazines tucked under his socks in his drawer and that Kate in the middle of love-play is often thinking about whether or not to stain the floorboards. This is good Ayckbourn comedy of recognition: the revelation on stage of the kind of things all of us (well most of us) admit to when we are alone with our partners.

But the joy of the Malcolm–Kate bedroom interludes is that Ayckbourn starts with the perfectly possible and nudges it a degree or two towards farce. The idea, for instance, of party-heaving hosts being caught out just as the guests begin to arrive is quite an old one (Bunuel's *The Discreet Charm of the Bourgeoisie* has them actually copulating in the back garden while the guests are feverishly knocking at the front door). But here Ayckbourn starts with the plausible – like Malcolm and Kate romping around as the doorbell rings – and then gently teases it so that poor Kate, naked under her bedroom towel, is forced to retreat under the covers as Trevor arrives to dump his coat on the bed. A minor domestic embarrassment also gives him a chance to establish straightway Trevor's total imperviousness to other people's predicaments.

Where Ayckbourn really scores as a comic master,

however, is in his ability to construct sight-gags that are relevant to character. He makes great play throughout with Malcolm's imagined gift for home-improvement (Ayckbourn always uses DIY as a moral test). Hints are dropped about the kitchen shelves he has put up that collapse under the weight of the cruet and matchstick banisters that yield under the delicate impress of a coat. But Ayckbourn's masterpiece is Malcolm's ham-fisted, small-hours construction of a surprise dressing-room table for Kate. What is astonishing is the comic mileage he gets out of one simple act.

He makes the point that Malcolm undertakes the shaky construct in a fit of pique while waiting up for the return of the peripatetic Trevor. He shows how Malcolm's bad temper and bull-necked impatience lead him to ignore the makers' complex instructions and do it his way. Then, when the table is unveiled, it turns out to be a ramshackle mess with a tilted surface and drawers that can only be opened with a deft blow of the fist. But Ayckbourn very cunningly delays its inevitable moment of collapse. Malcolm, in the act of sandpapering, falls fast asleep under his own wobbly construction and one half-expects him to wake up with a start, bang his head on the table and bring about its decline and fall. But Ayckbourn is cleverer than that. Because what he does is to make the returning Trevor the architect of destruction who, in trying to even out the table-top, causes the whole rickety structure to fall to pieces. This is much, much more than a beautifully rhythmed gag. It also becomes a symbol of Trevor's ability to destroy everything he touches – with, of course, the best will in the world – and of Ayckbourn's own ability to make points about character through visual metaphor.

To be honest, I find the dramatic temperature drops slightly when we move to Nick and Jan's. This is partly because the joke of Nick being confined to bed with a badly strained back has not got too many places to go. We have Nick dropping his book and being unable to move, Jan being caught under him in what looks like a compromising sexual position, the agony of Trevor invading the bedroom while Nick lies prone, the self-importance of the middle-management figure (always Ayckbourn's least favourite character) expecting dawn calls from America which turn out to be people in pursuit of Trevor. Ayckbourn certainly gives us a clear picture of the faintly hygienic, businesslike Nick–Jan alliance haunted by the shadow of Trevor as Jan's previous lover. The joke of the hyper-active man lying in bed in semi-agony, however, has not much possibility of extension.

Trevor and Susannah are a brilliant study in peripatetic selfishness, in the ability to live in cocooned isolation from the consequences of one's behaviour. Trevor, whose sentences go trailing off in mid-air like wisps of cigarette smoke, dottily believes that he will be welcome if he calls on Nick at three in the morning to apologise for kissing his wife at a party. Susannah drives through her in-laws' house in an emotional chariot and, after a particularly tormenting, caterwauling dream, says to Delia, 'I hope I haven't woken you'. (I am reminded of a journey I once made on a second-class London–Edinburgh sleeper with an incontinent Scotsman who, after several hazardous and noisy journeys to the bathroom in the course of the night, brightly remarked to me as we achieved Waverley Station during an ashen dawn, 'Excellent journey. You didn't disturb me once last night'.) Trevor and Susannah have the narcissism of the neurotic, the ruthlessness of the vulnerable, the total insensitivity to others of those who register their own emotional disturbances with seismic precision; and they are two of Ayckbourn's best creations in that we could all put a name to their real-life counterparts.

There are many other strands to this technically flawless play. One is Ayckbourn's knack, even with only three bedrooms and four couples, of reminding us of the existence of an off-stage world: you believe totally, for instance, in Malcolm and Kate's downstairs party where the guests include Dick and Lottie (fresh from *Absurd Person Singular*) and Gordon and Marge (direct from *Absent Friends*). Another is the easy rhythm of the cross-cutting from bedroom to bedroom which gives the action an unusual flow and suggests events may be developing in one room during our temporary absence. A third is Ayckbourn's aesthetic taste in leaving things to our imagination: a lesser writer would almost certainly show you Malcolm's reaction to the wanton ruination of his rigged-up dressing-table whereas he permits us to envisage the apoplectic fury. What makes this one of the best plays of the 1970s is partly that it leaves behind an ineradicable comic image, which proves that three beds are better than one, and partly that what Ayckbourn has to say about the blithe inconsiderateness of the suffering marries perfectly with his way of saying it. By this stage, his technical mastery was its height. The question was how much further he could go in exploring domestic destructiveness.

5

Winter Solstice

By the mid-1970s Ayckbourn was in an enviable position. Master of his own house in Scarborough. Virtually assured that almost everything he wrote would transfer to London (usually at the hands of Michael Codron). Endlessly done in rep, to whom his small-cast, one-set plays were a godsend. Performed throughout the world. He had it made.

What makes him an artist rather than a commercial pot-boiler, however, is that he was not content simply to go on turning out the mixture as before. He was never, I believe, purely an escapist comic writer: even a decade before in *Relatively Speaking* it had been a failure in marital communication that had made the wheels go round. As time went by, Ayckbourn grew in confidence and felt free to shed the high-wire pyrotechnics that people had come to expect of him. *Absent Friends* was the turning point: the play that proved he could handle tragic themes within a comic framework and hold an audience's undivided attention. Between the winter of 1976 and that of 1978 he went still further in a trio of plays (*Just Between Ourselves, Ten Times Table, Joking Apart*) of which only the middle one could remotely be described as a romp.

Ayckbourn in his introduction to the plays ascribes their prevailing darkness to the conditions under which they were written; to the fact that he was not sitting down in late spring to do a summer-season piece but composing in December for performance in January because the Library Theatre had evolved towards a twelve-month playing pattern: *Just Between Ourselves* was the first play to break the mould:

> As is customary, I wrote mainly at night – but this was my first experience of tackling a play while the North Sea storms hurtled round the house, slates cascaded from the roof and metal chimney cowlings were bounced off parked cars below my window, rebounding hither and thither like demented pinballs. Not surprisingly, the result was a rather sad (some say a rather savage) play with themes concerned with total lack of understanding, with growing old and with spiritual and mental collapse.

All of which is fascinating. But I have a hunch that Ayckbourne in these winter plays wanted to see how far he could push the comic form, how far he could go in absorbing themes of breakdown and despair, how much he could reverse the expectations that those increasingly familiar words 'the new Ayckbourn' inevitably aroused. In his seventeen years as a dramatist, he had never ceased to experiment with the possibilities of theatrical form. Now, in his maturity, he was also keen to experiment with content.

'Just Between Ourselves'

That experiment takes the form in *Just Between Ourselves* (which opened in Scarborough in January 1976 and came to the Queens Theatre, London, in 1977) of an uncompromising study of uncomprehending destructiveness: we ruin other people's lives, says Ayckbourn, and the tragedy is that we do not even know we are doing it.

Set on four successive birthdays in the course of a year, the play takes as its central figure Dennis, a bullish hearty who spends most of his spare time in his garage disastrously tinkering at various do-it-yourself projects. Dennis's reaction to life's problems is a blustering laugh: a laugh that keeps all emotion, fear, panic and sensitivity at bay and that prevents him seeing that his wife Vera (addressed by the patronising dimunitive of Vee) is breaking down. Vera's problems are caused partly by emotional neglect, the lack of any real function and the poisonous presence in the house of Dennis's mother determined to maintain her hold over her son. Unusually, Ayckbourn introduces a sub-plot that parallels the main one. Another couple, Neil and Pam, initially come round to look at the second-hand Morris Minor entombed in Dennis's garage. They become more and more implicated in Dennis and Vera's life, not least because Neil, weak, impotent, indecisive, cannot begin to understand why his own wife, an intelligent woman tied to the house by her son, is both desperate and unfulfilled. Pam, however, retains her rage whereas Vera, at the last, is driven into a dreadful, vegetable-like, catatonic state which Dennis greets with his usual blustery cheeriness.

To me the play is a bleak, mordant, biting tragi-comedy about what Terence Rattigan once called the real *vice anglais*: fear of expressing emotion. It is a quality that maims English males but that certainly attracts English dramatists. Rattigan himself handled it beautifully in *The Deep Blue Sea* where the blithe, golfing Freddie Page was totally bewildered by the emotional and sexual demands of his mistress, Hester Collyer. Simon Gray in *Otherwise Engaged* also showed that it can take the form of a cool, distancing irony that keeps people at arm's length. Ayckbourn here deals with emotion buried under a camouflage of cachinnation. For me the key line in the play comes when Dennis is cornered in the garage by a suddenly amorous Pam who cries, 'Presumably you've still got feelings' to which Dennis replies, 'Not if I can help them, I haven't'. Needless to say, he covers his confusion with a laugh.

Dennis is, in many ways, a monster. But he is also a victim. Ayckbourn makes it clear, with great skill, that heredity and environment have conspired to do for him. At first he seems a rather bovine, comic figure with a passion for DIY accompanied (as with Malcolm in *Bedroom Farce*) by total incompetence: the garage side door is permanently stuck, the up-and-over door will not budge and the Morris Minor he tries to flog to Neil is not only immoveable but also virtually unstartable. But his broad-bottomed, Naked Ape insensitivity is quickly displayed when he parades his wife's clumsiness in front of Neil:

> DENNIS: If I told you, Mr Andrews, the things my wife had caught with her elbow . . .
> VERA: (*shy and embarrassed*): All right.
> DENNIS: You would not believe it, Mr Andrews, cups, saucers, dinner plates, radio sets . . .
> NEIL: Really.
> DENNIS: Whole tray of glasses.
> VERA: Dennis . . .

DENNIS: And that's just for this month. You ever want a
demolition job doing, Mr Andrews, she's your
woman (*He laughs. Neil joins in half-heartedly. Vera
less so still.*)

Before you can pin Dennis down as a first-class brute,
however, you begin to learn something of his background
from his mother, who invades his garage sanctum. You
deduce that he must have been totally neglected by his
father who spent most of his waking hours in *his* garage,
'hammering away, making little things'. Not only that but
the father is brandished in front of him as a paragon of
creativity, tidiness, good order. Without indulging in
penny-in-the-slot psychology, Ayckbourn hints that
Dennis is the victim of a negligent, self-absorbed,
miserable father; that he has ruinously transferred all his
affection to his domineering mother; and that this Oedipal
relationship has squeezed out any hope of a normal
relationship with his wife, Vera, who is waving as she
drowns.

But Ayckbourn's talent is for showing rather than
telling: he does not give us a lecture about the
strangulatory hold of Dennis's mother but demonstrates it
in action. He does this largely through a biliously comic
birthday-party tea at the end of the first act in which
everyone tries to maintain a stoic indifference to Vera's
butter-fingered, nerve-shattered helplessness as she spills
cups and saucers and sends sugar flying in the air. It is
another of those Ayckbourn scenes that catches you
between wind and water not knowing whether to laugh or
cry.

Julian Jebb sent one's mind to the right place when he
said that Ayckbourn's 'use of props is equalled only by
Osborne'. There is a great scene in *The Entertainer* when

Phoebe castigates Archie Rice's father for devouring a cake she had specially prepared for her son expected home from Cyprus but actually killed in action. Oddly enough Constance Chapman, who had once played Phoebe in *The Entertainer*, also played mother Marjorie in *Just Between Ourselves*; and this time it was Vera's failure to bake a cake for Dennis's birthday that provoked the storm in a teacup. Bundled around like a stuffed dummy and parked just out of the wind at Dennis's gruesome alfresco party, Marjorie nags and chatters on unforgivingly about Vera's sin of omission. 'Ever since he was a little boy, he's always had his cake. Even when your father was dying, Dennis, I still made you your cake.' A small enough incident, you might think; but first-rate dramatists like Ayckbourn and Osborne can invest the seemingly trivial with great emotional significance and here the mother's obsession with the unbaked cake reveals an enormous amount about her inability to accept her son's maturity.

Dennis, in short, is another Ayckbourn example of arrested development: a shaggy, corduroyed blunderer ruined by an omnicompetent father, with whom he unconsciously competes, and a dreadnought, domineering mother who only achieves happiness when Vera is reduced to silence and she can resume her role as surrogate-wife. It is a textbook Freudian case; but it is a measure of the play's success that such thoughts only come to you afterwards. What you see is Dennis maniacally tinkering (even the electric kettle he repairs blows up in his mother's face), arranging surprise treats for his mum that also backfire, financially ruining Neil by encouraging him to invest his savings in some dodgy speculator, and constantly kidding himself that his wife Vera is on the mend.

Ayckbourn dramatises pain and incomprehension and leaves us with memorable images. But, although he is never doctrinaire or partisan, he does in this play show a rare understanding of the female viewpoint. He himself has said that he does not like overt politicising. 'Of course one can write a play about women's liberation – it's a very important topic – but I don't think it's very satisfying when they stand on a chair and tell the men in the audience that they're pigs. And that's where I differ from agit-prop theatre in that I hate being told things.' But although he never stoops (or rises, some would say) to preaching, there is an implicit feminism running through his work and nowhere more so than in *Just Between Ourselves* – a title, incidentally, that refers in part to Dennis's habit of having little masculine *tête-à-têtes* with Neil.

In this play he gives us a vivid picture of waste of female potential. Pam, a former office supervisor once in charge of twenty-five girls at a time, is now a mutinous housewife in charge of a son and a sexually inadequate husband. She yearns for something more, both professionally and personally: a degree course or even escape with Dennis, the cavalier laugher. She does not get it, however, because she has become mired in a kind of rancorous frustration. Vera, who once worked in Safeways, is meanwhile handicapped not merely by her own insecurity but by a fortyish feeling that, in her underqualified state, it is too late to get another job. Ayckbourn is fair enough to see that women can break out of the domestic trap if they try; but is also sympathetic enough to see the poignant plight of the stagnating middle-aged woman whose will and energy have been subtly eroded.

Ayckbourn makes many advances in this remarkable play: towards the handling of tragic material, towards extending pity to the destroyer as well as the destroyed, towards showing how age and time themselves become corrupters of purpose. But nothing in the play better demonstrates Ayckbourn's new tragi-comic finesse than the scene in which Vera comes to Dennis's lair in search of succour: her desperation confronts, with hideous irony, his emotional deafness.

VERA: It's just – I think I need help, Dennis.

DENNIS: How do you mean help?

VERA: From you. I don't think I can manage much longer unless I get your help.

DENNIS: Help. What way? With mother? Do you mean mother?

VERA: Partly. No, not just her. You never seem to be here, Dennis.

DENNIS: What do you mean? I'm here. I'm home as much as most men. Probably more than most men.

VERA: Yes, but you're out here, aren't you?

DENNIS: Not all the time.

VERA: Most of the time.

DENNIS: Well I'm doing things. For the house. I mean you're welcome to come out here too. There's nothing to stop you if you want to talk. Talk things over.

VERA: But we've got a home, Dennis. I spend all day trying to make it nice. I don't want to spend the evening sitting in a garage.

DENNIS: Oh come on.

VERA: I mean what's the point of my doing everything. I mean what's the point. I need help, Dennis.

DENNIS: Yes, but don't you see, you're not being clear Vee. You say help but what sort of help do you mean?

VERA: Just help. From you.

DENNIS: Yes. Well, look, tell you what. When you've got a moment, why don't you sit down, get a bit of paper and just make a little list of all the things you'd like me to help you with. Things you'd like me to do,

things that need mending or fixing and then we can
talk about them and see what I can do to help. All
right?
(*Vera does not reply.*)
How about that, Vee? All right? Does that suit you?
(*Vera moves to the door.*)
Vee?
(*Vera goes slowly out and into the house.*)
Vee. Vee.

I quote the scene in full because it strikes me as a
masterly bit of writing: emotional urgency on one side is
met by a non-comprehending perplexity on the other. One
notices, for instance, the sad reiteration of the word 'help';
but to Dennis the word's reverberations are to do with
mending and fixing rather than the spirit and the soul,
areas in which he is a total stranger. And his last, pathetic
utterances of that appalling diminutive 'Vee' create
a sharp impression of a man wandering in a fog of
incomprehension like a tourist in a Dartmoor mist.

My only cavil would be that Ayckbourn never tells us
what either Dennis or Neil do for a living: people's
professions are very much part of their lives and one longs
to know how these emotional and sexual cripples survive in
the world outside. But this is a small flaw in a work that
demonstrates the spiritual impoverishment that often
accompanies home improvement, the terrifying demands
of motherhood, the Englishman's unfeeling treatment of
his wife as some kind of labour-saving, domestic appliance
and, above all, the tragedy of what E. M. Forster called
'the under-developed heart'. This is Ayckbourn at his
wintriest; but, after seeing the play performed, one feels
that he caught something that is true about many of our
lives.

Alan Ayckbourn

'Ten Times Table'

Winter writing did not automatically mean gloom and doom for Ayckbourn. *Ten Times Table* (which opened in Scarborough in January 1977 and in London in April 1978) is a reasonably light-hearted study of committee-itis. 'The play', says Ayckbourn in his introduction, 'could be described, I suppose, as a predominantly sedentary farce with faintly allegorical overtones. In more innocent days, it would probably have been sub-titled a romp.'

Actually the story goes that during London rehearsals of *Ten Times Table* (the first play of his own that Ayckbourn had directed in the West End) a cleaner remarked: 'The trouble with this play is that it starts out as comedy and ends up as farce'. Which just goes to show that there are many mute, inglorious Tynans around London. The play's first half is a barbed, accurate, funny account of committee-table manners based, as Ayckbourn makes clear in his preface, on his own experiences in 1976 when the Scarborough company he directs was due to move from the Public Library to the Boys' Grammar School. The second act is a boisterous, knockabout account of a pageant that degenerates into a violently intemperate battle with present-day left- and right-wing ideologues fighting it out in a risible echo of the historical event they are celebrating. Along the way, there are plenty of laughs; but Ayckbourn's first real venture into public issues leaves something to be desired.

The best feature of the play is Ayckbourn's demonstration of committee-itis: the way some people blossom and others dwindle when formally seated round a table. A group of people come together to plan a pageant based on a historical incident known as the Massacre of the Pendon Twelve: the story of a local revolt by agricultural

1. Alan Ayckbourn.

2. *Bedroom Farce* at the Lyttelton Theatre, 1977, directed by Alan Ayckbourn and Peter Hall. Left to right: Stephen Moore (Trevor), Susan Littler (Kate), Derek Newark (Malcolm).

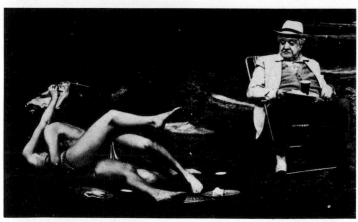

3. *Sisterly Feelings* at the Olivier Theatre, 1980, directed by Alan Ayckbourn and Christopher Morahan. Left to right: Selina Cadell (Brenda), Greg Hicks (Melvyn), Andrew Cruickshank (Dr Ralph Matthews).

4. *Confusions* at the Apollo Theatre, 1976, with Derek Fowlds, John Alderton and Pauline Collins.

5. *Way Upstream* at the Lyttelton Theatre, 1982, directed by Alan Ayckbourn. Left to right: Susan Fleetwood (June), Julie Legrand (Emma).

6. *Table Manners* at the Globe Theatre, 1974, with (left to right) Mark Kingston, Felicity Kendal, Penelope Wilton, Tom Courtenay, Michael Gambon and Penelope Keith.

7. *The Story So Far* at Scarborough, 1970. Left to right: Stephanie Turner, Piers Rogers, Elizabeth Sladen, Heather Stoney and Joe Dunlop.

8. *The Sparrow* at Scarborough, 1967, with Robert Powell, Heather Stoney and Pamela Craig.

9. *Mr Whatnot* at the Library Theatre, Scarborough, 1976. Left to right: Bob Eaton (Herbert), Robin Herford (Cecil), Diane Bull (Amanda), Wendy Murray (Agnes) and Heather Stoney (Lady Slingsby-Craddock).

10. *Absurd Person Singular,* Scarborough, 1972, with Matyelok Gibbs, Piers Rogers, Christopher Godwin and Philippa Urquhart.

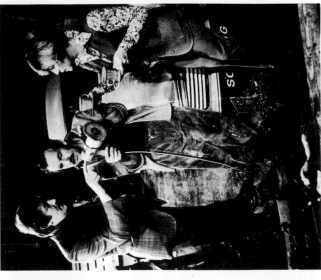

11. *Absurd Person Singular* at the Criterion Theatre, 1973, with Anna Calder Marshall and David Burke.

12. *Just Between Ourselves* at the Queen's Theatre, 1977, with Michael Gambon, Colin Blakeley and Rosemary Leach.

workers crushed by a brutal militia. Ayckbourn deftly sketches in the committee-types. There is Ray Dixon, a shopowner for whom chairing the committee is a natural extension of civic power, and his wife, Helen, venomously hostile to anything leftish. There is Councillor Evans, a prissy, bureaucrat bachelor who puts his ineffectual energy into good works and brings in his wake a deaf, octogenarian mother. There is Eric, a Marxist comprehensive school teacher, with an inaudibly shy common-law wife, who quickly attracts the affection of Sophie, an emotionally-accident-prone dog-breeder. There is Lawrence Adamson, a maudlin, semi-coherent drunk with a collapsing marriage; and, eventually co-opted, there is Tim, Sophie's crypto-fascist, fanatical, pistol-packing brother. Ayckbourn's method of characterisation is here rather like one of those games where you join up a sequence of numbers to produce a complete figure. He leaves it to us to make the necessary connections.

Ayckbourn's frustrating months of sitting on a committee himself were clearly not wasted. The early scenes capture the mix of punctiliousness and absurdity that hover over many such local groups. The way the lights keep going out in the dilapidated Swan Hotel Ballroom; the way Councillor Evans fusses over the punctuation and spelling in the minutes; the appointing of his almost totally deaf mother to take the minutes; the fishing through diaries to find out when one can next hold a meeting; even the sidelong use of the gathering to do a little local business with Dixon complaining of the non-delivery of his track-lighting from Adamson – all this is both true and funny and strikes sparks of recognition. Ayckbourn makes the point that ordinary, sane people somehow become translated by committee work.

So what is wrong with the play? My own feeling is that

119

Ayckbourn draws too broad and obvious a distinction between Helen Dixon, the fur-coated, right-wing snob and Eric, the knee-jerk, Dave Spartish Marxist who is part of the lumpen-Polytechnic. It is a little hard to believe that Eric, who is no closet leftie, would have been invited on to the committee in the first place. And, after Helen Dixon has attacked the agricultural martyrs they are supposed to be celebrating and after Eric has called her 'a stupid bourgeois bitch', it is a little hard to accept that he would have been earnestly asked to stay. Of course, he has to stay in order to stoke the plot. Eric exploits the pageant as an excuse for a political rally in which he will play the chief martyr, Jonathan Cockle, and make tub-thumping denunciations of the capitalists. Meanwhile the Dixons, Evans, the sloshed Adamson and Sophie's lunatic brother form a rival faction to ensure fair play for the militia. But in the best of Ayckbourn things do not happen merely to keep the plot boiling.

Not only are Helen and Eric rather broadly drawn. I also feel Ayckbourn shows a crucial difference in attitude towards them. Helen is seen as an uppity, toffee-nosed housewife who gets her just deserts at the end of the play when she is happily banged by a drunken, bearded, Slough-born leftie: a process that, on the evidence, she seems quite to enjoy. But Eric (like all figures of the far left in popular drama) is an outright villain who uses the pageant for his own personal ego trip, keeps two women contentedly in tow but, when defeated, turns on them in snarling hatred: 'Get away from me. Both of you. Leave me alone. You pair of bourgeois, middle-class housewives. They haven't won yet. They haven't heard the last of Jonathan Cockle.'

I do not dispute Ayckbourn's right to pitch into the Marxists; any more than I dispute his right to knock the vacillations and compromises of the Pendon burghers. But I think, for dramatic purposes, one needs to apply the same rigorous standards to both. Helen is actually proved right in her analysis of Marxist tactics when she deplores the idea of one group organising the Pendon Twelve and the other the military: 'That's how they work. That's the way they gain their power. By dividing people up.' And even though she, quite literally, gets her come-uppance, she is morally vindicated. It is, of course, true that the loony far right is exemplified by the gun-toting Tim; but even he is viewed largely as a crackpot eccentric. Christopher Godwin, who played the role both in Scarborough and London, left behind an ineradicable image of a manic English Clouseau constantly making lethal darts at curtains in search of hidden lefties. Tim is a figure from farce (though his cry, 'They're scum, Dixon, scum' curiously echoes Somerset Maugham's famous verdict on the new class of redbrick scholar epitomised by Kingsley Amis's Jim Dixon) whereas Eric is, in Peter Stothard's words, 'actively disliked by author and audience alike'. Ayckbourn is a bad hater: really to put down the Erics of this world, I think one has to know them better.

It would be silly to deny that the play does make one laugh. The sight of Audrey Evans, the deaf octogenarian playing old musical comedy numbers while the Massacre of the Pendon Twelve degenerates into an ugly brawl, is very funny in the traditional manner of characters oblivious to chaos: it is rather like the pianist who keeps on pumping out melodies in Westerns while the saloon breaks up all around him. Ayckbourn also gets some characteristically funny visual gags out of the spectacle of short-sighted burghers dressed up as militia men and creates a genuine sense of community, not least through reference to the Pendon Players who once did *Moby Dick*: 'Yes', says Councillor Evans, 'the one about the whale. It was very successful. In fact, many people preferred it to the film.' Quite so.

But although the play makes one laugh, it has not at the end told us much other than that committees give nonentities a spurious power and often cause respected pillars of the community to crumble. With hindsight, one cannot help enjoying the joke whereby Audrey Evans comes up with a new subject for a pageant. 'Did you know, when the Romans first arrived in Britain, they met a very strong pocket of resistance round here. From the Britons. Just on the edge of Pendon.'

Although this seems like an uncanny prognostication about *The Romans in Britain*, it also reminds one that Ron Hutchinson wrote a piece, *The Irish Play*, which also showed a committee factionally at work and which also ended up with a pageant beset by strife and dwindling into chaos. But whereas Hutchinson's desire was to give us a tangible, microcosmic image of modern Ireland, Ayckbourn's motive seems to be to give us a rather generalised picture of class conflict and to point up the way committee procedures transform people, promoting some, depressing others. I do not want to be harsh on a play that makes me laugh; at the same time I do not think it has the questing truth of top-flight Ayckbourn.

'Joking Apart'

After this *divertissement*, the tone darkens once again in *Joking Apart* (first seen at the Stephen Joseph Theatre-in-the-Round, Scarborough, in January 1978 and at the Globe in London in 1979). Which is slightly ironic considering the play's origins. 'Somebody said "Why don't you write about a really nice couple? I'm fed up with all these bloody awful marriages.'' I said ''Yes, I really must get this couple together.'' ' The result is a play about the unjust distribution of human luck and about the devouring nature of the gifted and fortunate: about the kind of people endowed with effortless flair who gobble up all the losers who drift into their orbit. Of course, the play touches on many other themes: the drift into middle age (the action covers a span of twelve years in which the characters move from their late twenties to their early forties), the ache of a failed marriage, the numbing awareness of one's own mediocrity, the seasonal rituals of English life. But what is striking is the way Ayckbourn, himself unusually gifted, portrays the unattractive aspects of those who win the glittering prizes and extends a lot of dramatic sympathy to the also-rans and failures.

In London, the play never proved very popular largely because it defied audience expectations: no great show of technical virtuosity, no revelation of character through farce, no continuum of laughter to offset the pain. Ayckbourn's own natural urge to dig deeper into character and be ever more bleakly truthful came into conflict with audience expectations. Hence the puzzled reaction to *Just Between Ourselves* and *Joking Apart*. What made the situation even more poignant was that Michael Codron, Ayckbourn's faithful West End producer, always seemed to get the 'darker' plays while the National Theatre, subsidised to the hilt, scooped up a natural audience-grabber like *Bedroom Farce*.

But *Joking Apart*, though caviare to the general, has a lot to recommend it: a basic psychological truth, a gradual revelation of character, a feeling for the inaudible and noiseless foot of time. By taking a twelve-year time-span Ayckbourn is able to chart the changes that take place in people's lives as they come into contact with Richard and Anthea, the dashing, golden duo to whom everything comes easy. At first, they seem like perfect hosts: charming, considerate, well-intentioned, likeable. At their Guy Fawkes party, they welcome a raw new vicar and his wife, Hugh and Louise Emerson, even when their monster-brat urinates on the fireworks. They are equally kind to Richard's self-delighted Finnish business partner and his wife, Sven and Olive Holmenson. And they are pointedly nice to Brian, an old chum desperately in love with Anthea, and his strident Canadian girl friend Melody. They ply people with soup and sausages, let off fireworks and build bonfires and generally behave like the ideal neighbours.

However Ayckbourn (Scarborough's Ibsen) is fascinated by the blithe destructiveness of the good. And we see this at work when Richard, with Anthea's encouragement, decides to tear down the fence that separates their house, the old vicarage, from the smaller, redbrick house occupied by the new vicar and his wife. His motives are generous: to provide a large communal garden space. But the effect is horrendous, particularly on the vicar's wife, who feels that her security, her privacy, her territory have been invaded. It is a strong dramatic image; and it reminds us that 'Do as you would be done by' is all very well except that other people's tastes may be different from yours. We begin to see that Richard and Anthea are steamrollering philanthropists who want everyone to be happy on their terms. Sven (who, in one of Ayckbourn's wittiest stage directions, 'nods approvingly at nature as he walks') sounds a warning note:

> SVEN: May I just say one thing? As friends, be careful of them.

HUGH: How do you mean?
SVEN: No. I'll say nothing more. Be careful. Beware.
    That's all. Goodnight to you.

The full irony of this comes in the second scene –
summer four years later – where it is Sven himself who
seems to be suffering most from Richard's cool, effortless
flair. Sven (particularly as played originally by Robert
Austin, a plumply-balding pouter pigeon) is one of
Ayckbourn's best characters: arrogant, measured, verbally
precise but growingly sympathetic as we realise that Finns
ain't what they used to be and that he cannot compete with
Richard's natural gifts. With some pathos he reveals to
Anthea his displeasure at Richard's habit of taking
unilateral decisions that could easily have bankrupted the
firm:

ANTHEA: Has he done that?
SVEN: Thank heavens, no. More through luck than good
    judgement, he has actually lost us very little. In fact,
    to be strictly accurate he has made us a little. In fact,
    he has made us quite a nice little sum and he has
    incidentally found us a new outlet for Swedish
    glassware. Nevertheless, these decisions were
    irrational, made without reference to known trading
    conditions, the present state of the world market or,
    more important, me.

Sven, you feel, has a case; yet the very placing of that last
phrase shows that his character is marred by a child-like
egoism. It is a sign of Ayckbourn's ever maturing skill that
he shows Sven to be smug, pompous, self-satisfied, proud
of his talent for tennis and his superiority to his wife as a
cook; and that, at the same time, he has the pathos that

accrues to all of Richard's victims. Ayckbourn's sympathy for the defeated and exploited (something you can trace right back to *Relatively Speaking*) extends also to the chumpish vicar who cannot get his sermons together, to his nervous, resentful wife and to Sven's spouse who is forced to be an admiring acolyte. My one doubt about this second scene is that Sven's devastatingly acute analysis of Richard and Anthea's talent for taking people over ('And they do it in this very pleasant way. In this friendly way. But the motive itself is the most selfish of human motives, the desire for power over other people') is a little too explicatory. Ayckbourn, through Sven, spells out almost too precisely what is wrong with Richard and Anthea so that the play becomes as much the proof of a thesis as the demonstration of a flaw.

The Second Act remedies this with a brilliant first scene on a wet Boxing Day four years later. Tennis is being played on a waterlogged court and Richard's effortless superiority is becoming ever more oppressive. Sven, totally emasculated, has been reduced to a gratuitous pen-pusher. The local vicar is forced by his Anthea-crowded wife to make a detour when they pass the house. What is more, he himself has mistaken Anthea's indiscriminate friendliness for something more and fallen in love with her. But the highlight of the act is quintessential Ayckbourn: a tennis match between Sven and Richard in which the former is attempting to retrieve his manhood and individuality. And, despite his wife hissing encouragement through the wire netting, he finally wins (we only ever see one side of the net but even that is quite a technical feat). At least in one area he has proved his superiority. Then, with immaculate timing, comes the revelation from another of Brian's disastrous girl friends that Richard has all the time been playing left-handed. Sven is shattered by Richard's kind cruelty: 'I see. At least you paid me the compliment of not hopping on one leg as well. Let's go in.'

The last scene whisks us on another four years to the eighteenth birthday of Debbie, Richard and Anthea's daughter. Lights are being strung up around the tennis-court. Loud-speakers are being installed. Richard and Anthea are advancing into golden (though still unmarried) early middle age. But everyone they have come into contact with is diminished. Sven is now a post-coronary semi-invalid. The vicar's wife has the artificial brightness of a drugged doll. Brian, a neutered tom who long ago fell in love with Anthea and whose life was blighted ever after, has now reached an age when he finds it harder to come up with another of his platonic girl friends. As all Richard and Anthea's friends gather for the party and make sad, embarrassed or footling speeches, Debbie bluntly asks her mum: 'Haven't you got any normal friends at all?'

ANTHEA: What on earth do you mean?
DEBBIE: Well, they're sort of lost looking.

This gets to the heart of the matter: that Richard and Anthea not only attract waifs and strays but also delight in them, indeed even turn people into them, because it reinforces their own good fortune. Ayckbourn leaves you feeling that it might almost be better to be a Sven or a Brian or a Louise because one has at least encountered some kind of human despair whereas Richard and Anthea sail through life on a cloud of unknowing.

Michael Frayn in his underrated 1971 play, *The Sandboy*, also dealt with the golden cocoon that surrounds the gifted and fortunate. Peter Shaffer in *Amadeus* showed mediocrity getting its revenge on the divinely talented. But *Joking Apart* is very much Ayckbourn's own

127

play: a sharp, perceptive, unyielding study of the destructiveness of human colonisation (you can never picture Richard and Anthea as guests – only as permanent hosts), the unknowing cruelty of life's winners, the whimsicality of luck. I have seen it objected that the work is too neat, tidy and structured for its own good as if this somehow lessened the pain. Indeed some people seem to resent the fact that someone as formally precise as Ayckbourn traffics in human misery. But the classic answer to that kind of charge was once supplied by W. H. Auden in a footnote on Tennyson:

It is interesting to speculate on the relation between the strictness and musicality of a poet's form and his own anxiety. It may well be, I think, that the more he is conscious of an inner disorder and dread, the more value he will place on tidiness in the work as a *defense*, as if he hoped that through his control of the means of expressing his emotions, the emotions themselves, which he cannot master directly, might be brought to order.

Something of that applies to Ayckbourn's mature work: a creeping disenchantment with man's unconscious inhumanity to man is balanced and contained by an exemplary comic form.

6

Onwards and Upwards

I hope so far I have established two absolute facts about Ayckbourn. One is that he is a serious writer with his own angle of vision on such matters as marriage, family life, tribal rituals, innocent destructiveness, male insensitivity and the success-ethic. Another is that he is a restless technical experimenter, always trying to increase the frontiers of the possible. In that sense, he is a theatre man through and through. Almost every other post-war British dramatist has flirted with cinema, television and radio, sometimes achieving a delightful consummation (or, in the case of movies, handsome compensation). Ayckbourn alone has achieved a living (and a pretty handsome one at that) out of the theatre. He is fascinated by what theatre can do. He is even more fascinated by showing that there is virtually nothing that it cannot do. I once suggested that 'if asked to write a farce for five, non-English-speaking unicyclists set in a broom-cupboard you feel he could do it'. I eagerly await his response to the challenge.

Looking at his amazing, indeed accelerating, output

since 1979 one finds him working in a variety of forms: comedy (*Sisterly Feelings, Season's Greetings*), farce (*Taking Steps*), lunch-time musical (*First Course, Second Helping, Me, Myself and I*), late-night revue (*Men on Women on Men*), full-scale musical play (*Suburban Strains, Making Tracks*), quasi-political allegory (*Way Upstream*), musical adaptation (*A Trip to Scarborough*) and what one might term multiple drama in the shape of *Intimate Exchanges* which has thirty different scenes which can be permutated to make sixteen different versions of the play. For most dramatists, that would be the work of a decade or more. For Ayckbourn, it amounts to no more than three years' output.

Such prodigious output is itself regarded as suspect. John Updike's Henry Bech, a writer who for years lives off the mystique of his non-productivity, is told by an admiring sister-in-law in *Bech is Back*, that 'Your paralysis was so beautiful. It was. . . . statuesque'. And it is quite true that a dramatist or novelist who reluctantly squeezes out a single work every decade like toothpaste coming out from the bottom of a tube is going to be more highly regarded than one who produces two or three major pieces a year. But Ayckbourn, who at a time and an age when he could be resting on a whole bower of laurels, instead chooses to go on experimenting, experimenting, experimenting like the obsessive Balzac hero of *The Quest for the Absolute* seeking the perfect elixir.

'Men on Women on Men'

This late-night revue, played at Scarborough in June 1978, consists of a series of sketches and songs (with music by Scarborough's resident composer, Paul Todd) that explore the old male-female jingle-jangle. The tone is light and jaunty; but the cumulative message is one of cryptic pessimism about the possibility of men and women ever achieving a proper, harmonious understanding. Thus in the first scene we see two couples squabbling over something as simple as ordering a round of drinks; and this leads into a song sequence in which the men lament: 'To think the romance of a boy meeting girl/Should finish up a comi-tragedy'; in which the women see themselves eternally settling for second-best and in which the two sexes finally concur:

> You've got to hand it to someone
> Whoever fixed the rules
> Of this mis-matched game
> Must have quite a sense of humour
> Saddling a man with woman
> Woman upon man.

Given (from Ayckbourn's past form) the likelihood of the message, what is instructive is the number of variations that he and Mr Todd manage to ring upon it. So we see a couple dining out and swapping Mittyesque images of their real selves; a recently-met and only-just-married boy and girl arriving at a honeymoon suite in Benidorm and still clinging to their precarious idealistic view of each other; two emotionally damaged men forswearing women until the next pretty one passes by; a trapped housewife making a tentative Saturday-night bid for freedom; one married couple non-communicating over breakfast and another edging into divorce. It all goes to prove Montaigne's dictum: 'Marriage is like a cage; one sees the birds outside desperate to get in, and those inside equally desperate to get out'.

But the revue is more than an indictment of marriage: it is a poised and poignant *cri de coeur* about the impossibility of men and women ever devising a way of living together. It is not, however, unconstructive. In a number laced with wit, it suggests the only sensible possibility is for some kind of biological merger of the sexes:

> Make a fearsome case
> To end this segregation
> And unify the nation.
> No more blacks or whites
> But merely grey hermaphrodites.

Under the joke, Ayckbourn is perhaps claiming that the only hope lies in eroding the notion of the manly man and the womanly woman; and that only when we get away from the usual self-deceptive stereotypes will there ever be any hope of sexual harmony. His play shows the ruinous nature of the way we love (and live) now. In this sparky, jaundiced little revue he implies there may just possibly be a way out.

'Sisterly Feelings'

There are no easy answers, however, in *Sisterly Feelings* (which began its life at Scarborough in January 1979 and moved to the National's Olivier Theatre in 1980). Ayckbourn calls it 'a related comedy': a neat joke since it is about sibling rivalry (two sisters competing for the same fella) and since, in Ayckbourn's words, 'four combinations of alternative versions are possible depending first on a toss of a coin at the end of the short prologue, then halfway through by a decision made by one or other of the sisters during the course of the action'. It is a play about choice. It is also one in which the actresses concerned have an element of choice. Even for Ayckbourn, this is a radical departure (though not wholly original since I recall, as a teenager, sitting on the jury of an American courtroom drama with two alternative endings depending on the verdict the jurors returned). The key question, however, is whether Ayckbourn's audacious technique meshes with his philosophy.

To answer that, one must first establish the complex structure. The play always begins with an eccentric, widowed doctor bringing his family, straight from his wife's funeral, to a favourite spot on Pendon Common (this time somewhere in Berkshire: Pendon gets about a bit). He has two daughters: Abigail, married to a rather stuffy businessman called Patrick, and Dorcas, a local-radio presenter attached to a scruffy radical poet called Stafford. Because Patrick drives off prematurely to a meeting, there is only one car to take the whole group (eight in all) home. And so one of the sisters is left to walk back with the suntanned, athletic Simon, their brother's fiancée's brother (still with me?). The sisters toss for it.

The second scene is a summer family picnic on Pendon Common. But two versions are possible. If Abigail won the toss, she is now in the throes of a passionate *affaire* with Simon but hotly pursued by husband Patrick: if Dorcas called right, she will now be partnered by Simon but with boy friend Stafford skulking in the bushes. An apocalyptic rainstorm ends the scene and the sisters are again faced with a choice: either to go home with their original partner or cycle off with Simon.

The next scene presents even more bold alternatives. If

Abigail keeps Simon (or indeed wrests him from Dorcas's clutches) we now see her having a would-be romantic night under canvas with him on the Common but one that ends with her realising that he is rather cautiously conventional and her nearly getting nabbed by the cops as she does an indecorous striptease to the glow of an upturned torch. If, on the other hand, Dorcas keeps Simon (or wrests him from Abigail) we are confronted by the annual cross-country derby in which she realises that her *beau ideal* is an emotional bully and in which she ends up rolling in the mud with the raffish Stafford. The final scene, however, always ends with a trip to the Common on the wedding-day of the sisters' brother, Melvyn, to his inarticulate fiancée. By this time Abigail and Dorcas, back with their original partners, are happily reunited.

So what actually does the four-in-one *Sisterly Feelings* say? This is Ayckbourn's answer.

It came out of giving too many interviews really where one tends to put together groups of facts conveniently. You know I would say 'Then I decided to leave Oxford Playhouse and go back to Scarborough to write plays'. I didn't decide any of those things really: the season finished and this happened or that happened. Circumstances did it and it was only afterwards that one put on the decision-making process. That's what it's saying in fact. The other thing I suppose it says is that it doesn't make all that much bloody difference anyway. Unlike a lot of plays which say you always get married to the wrong person, it also says you get married to the right person: if you don't like them, it's probably your fault for being the sort of person you are. You've got the person you deserve. I think Abigail has Patrick because she needs Patrick; and Patrick does for her what a big, glorious bronzed idiot can get nowhere near doing for her.

That seems to me perceptive, even profound: that our partners are often a reflection of our own inadequacies. But, in performance, the play does pose one real problem: that Abigail's variations are much more interesting than Dorcas's because she is married. A woman dithering between a dull husband and a bronzed lover is far more fascinating than one caught between two boyfriends; simply because more is at stake. That, in itself, says quite a lot about our nostalgic affection for the iron proprieties of marriage: we still find adultery more exciting than a choice of lovers. But it also has to be said that Abigail's nocturnal Bacchic frenzy on Pendon Common is far funnier than Dorcas and Stafford sorting out their problems in the middle of a cross-country race: for once, you feel that Ayckbourn's natural well-spring of invention is running a little dry.

But I am not sure that the play, even in its four alternative versions, does prove that we get the partners we deserve. All it really shows is that Simon, the bronzed athlete just back from a supposedly buccaneering trip to Africa, is on closer inspection a bit of an idiot. We gradually learn that he never actually saw the African bush, that he alone was made redundant by his firm out there, that he has come back to teach P.E. and that he cannot stand jokes against himself. Like the athletic Peter in *Time and Time Again*, he is a bit of a dullard (for all his well known love of cricket, Ayckbourn always shows sympathy to non-games-playing weeds like Stafford). But suppose Simon had turned out to be dashing, adventurous, imaginative, intelligent, a real catch? Where would

Ayckbourn's philosophy be then? What *Sisterly Feelings* really proves, I suspect, is that we hasten back to our partners when the alternative is even worse.

Cavils aside, *Sisterly Feelings* does play some brilliant variations on familiar Ayckbourn themes. As John Peter pointed out, the unvarying ending makes the point that 'the family remains each time as we first saw it, in full possession of its victims, its obsessions and its insecurities'. Moreover the two family picnics show the purgatorial nature of English tribal rituals. We set out for a communal alfresco celebration and what happens? Endless arguments about who has got Stafford's vegetarian sandwich, whether there are too many sardine-and-cucumbers, who drinks orange squash or tea. Out of such trivia, Ayckbourn builds a devastating picture of the lurking rattiness of most family get-togethers; and, against the background of rows over the butties, the sister who lost Simon first time round is trying to steal him back. This, we recognise, is what life is like; passion erupting from a texture of family irritation.

Seeing the plays twice (or even four times if you are a really dedicated Ayckbourn freak) also underscores their hidden truths. The way, for instance, sibling rivalry gives way to sisterly possessiveness when it comes to protecting Melvyn, an underachieving medical student, from the clutches of fiancée Brenda. And indeed the way Abigail and Dorcas turn into a mini-Goneril and Regan when they discuss their wayward father and his habit of communing with his dead wife:

ABIGAIL: . . . The other day I heard him telling her a
funny story. Roaring with laughter. Him that is. And
then there's some days he refuses to wear socks and at
least once a week he wants his bed moving round

because of the way the earth's rotating . . . I mean he can't be senile, can he, not yet? He's not old enough. He's only just seventy . . .

Only when you see the plays from more than one angle do you also grasp the way each sister, when left alone with Simon in the second scene, delicately undermines the other. Dorcas puts the boot in by implying that Abigail makes ravenous demands on people and is invariably disappointed; while Abigail says of Dorcas that: 'The Dorcas you see there is the total Dorcas. What you see is what you get.' Not only is this psychologically plausible: it also prepares the ground for the swapping of partners at the end of the scene.

But what, I am convinced, gives *Sisterly Feelings* its life and vitality is not merely that it introduces an element of chance and risk into the set patterns of drama (performances which were left genuinely open apparently had an edge denied to those where the audience knew the version they were going to see in advance) but Ayckbourn's sprightly contrast between characters still capable of pursuing their fancy and those locked into some immutable Jonsonian humour. The peripheral figures here are marvellous. Ralph, the dotty septuagenarian doctor, who advises his rapidly dwindling patients to take off their socks and live. Len, his brother-in-law, a ramrod-backed *flic* obsessed with the breakdown of society: 'If I related to you the statistics regarding car thefts for one month in this area, it would horrify you. Horrify you. We don't release the true figures. The general public would panic.' Patrick, the seething cuckold, outraged less by his wife's defection than by the fact that she has nicked a bottle of his prize Chateau Latour 62 for her illicit camping-trip. (Michael Gambon endowed this last character at the Olivier with a wonderful glint of danger and menace under the camel-hair-coated cool.)

The truth about *Sisterly Feelings* in the end is that the technique is more seductive than the philosophy is convincing: in that sense, it is not on the level of *The Norman Conquests* where the two work in perfect harmony. But Ayckbourn the craftsman has spoiled us for choice. We now begin to nitpick about the relative merits of one work as against another when what is really remarkable is his constant attempt to find out what you can do on a stage. For years comedy in the English theatre has been confined to rooms, to petty infidelities, to whether Jack sleeps with Jill or Joan, to an upper-middle-class or aristocratic life-style which the audience gazed at with lumpen envy, to a world in which people did nothing more athletic than stroll over to the drinks table for another G. and T. or Scotch-on-the-rocks.

Ayckbourn's productivity has, in a way, made us blasé. We have forgotten just how much he personally has pushed out the boat and the frontiers so that comedy can deal with recognisable people and encompass attempted suicide, personality destruction, business opportunism – not to mention cricket, tennis, camping-trips, lunches, dinners, teas, picnics, parties and, in formal terms, off-stage action, on-stage choice and different permutations of a single situation. Ayckbourn found English comedy in the 1960s in an impoverished state of attrition in which conscience made sub-Cowards of us all. By his daring, he has proved that there is absolutely nothing comedy cannot tackle; and, however much *Sisterly Feelings* may turn out in the end to be Abigail's party, we should judge it in the rich context of Ayckbourn's own pioneering comic excursions.

'Taking Steps'

Unpredictable, capricious, uncataloguable as ever, Ayckbourn turned next not to the bleak comedy one might have expected but to downright farce in the shape of *Taking Steps* (first seen in Scarborough in September 1979 and at the Lyric Theatre in London a year later). Farce itself is a genre about which much ink has been spilt, often to good purpose. John Mortimer, for instance, hit the nail firmly on the head when he wrote:

> The world of farce is necessarily square, solid, respectable and totally sure of itself: only so can it be exploded. There is nothing comical about a trembling masochist being kicked on the behind or a sprightly and permissive collection of Swedish teenagers being caught in the wrong bedroom. These events must occur only to the most dignified and moral persons. It is impossible to be funny about funny people.

Too true. I remember once seeing a Bamber Gascoigne farce, *The Feydeau Farce Festival of Nineteen Nine*, which was about a group of actors in a theatre at the source of the Amazon: for all Mr Gascoigne's invention, it was not terribly funny because the actors had precious little dignity to lose in the first place. The only person to circumvent this rule has been Michael Frayn who in *Noises Off* has written a funny farce about the theatre because he shows what happens when the hairline precision of a farce performance is itself dislocated: one step out of place and the whole delicate artefact goes spinning into chaos.

So farce needs to be built on a base of propriety. But under that all kinds of demons can lurk; and Eric Bentley tapped the dark aggression of farce in a brilliant essay in *The Life of the Drama*:

> Farce in general offers a special opportunity: shielded by delicious darkness and seated in warm security, we enjoy the privilege of being totally passive while on stage our most treasured, unmentionable wishes are fulfilled before our eyes by the most violently active human beings that ever sprang from the human imagination. In that application of the formula which is bedroom farce, we savour the adventure of adultery, ingeniously exaggerated in the highest degree, and all without taking the responsibility or suffering the guilt. Our wives may be with us leading the laughter.

Taking Steps abides pretty well by these ground rules. Roland, a wealthy bucket manufacturer who drinks like a fish, is about to buy a leaky Norman cavern of a house from a twerpy builder with the help of Tristram, a juvenile solicitor who can never complete a coherent sentence. At the same time Roland's wife, Lizzie, is making a rather indecisive leap for freedom in order to get back to her career as a show-dancer, and Roland's brother-in-law, Mark, who only has to start speaking to send his auditors to sleep, is trying to cope with a suicidal fiancée also determined to get her freedom. So we have respectable people (with the exception perhaps of Lizzie) suffering all manner of adversity. We also have innocence sexually triumphant since Tristram, in the course of an eventful Friday night and Saturday morning, manages to get into bed with the play's two women.

Ayckbourn is never one simply to play by the rules. His most original stroke in this play is putting the attic, the master bedroom, the living room and two staircases on to the same stage space and the same plane so that we see action happening in them concurrently. Obviously this makes for instant sight-gags like people going up and down stairs while, in reality, staying on the same level. But it also provides the chance for simultaneous farcical action with Lizzie, for instance, coquettishly prepared to leap into her marital bed (in fact, occupied by Tristram who thinks he is seeing the family ghost) while a drunken, pill-filled Roland is sleeping in the attic and mouthing the Anvil Chorus at the same time as Kitty, his brother-in-law's fiancée, is trapped in a cupboard wedged in by his bed. The house itself thus becomes a character in the farce: a gaunt, ghostly, doomy, looming Victorian pile in which two beds are better than one, in which the audience can see people trying to make their ineffectual escape down imaginary flights of stairs and in which separate crises can erupt a few feet away from each other. It is a return to the expertise of *How The Other Half Loves* in which two overlapping households existed chic-by-jowl.

This gives a corkscrew-twist to the usual farcical techniques, but Ayckbourn manages to make this a farce *about* something: specifically the question of freedom and sexual choice. Lizzie, an erotic and funny self-deceiver who talks about her career as if she were once a star dancer with the Bolshoi rather than in the back row of a TV line-up, is forever trying to escape from husband, house and security but cannot quite make the decisive move. Kitty, a semi-coherent neurotic who gets trapped for the night in a cupboard, meets her perfect verbal match in Tristram and for them it is non-communication at first sight. Kitty escapes through a *coup de foudre*: Lizzie is the classic ditherer who cannot make up her mind whether to stay or go-go.

Dedicated to Ben Travers, *Taking Steps* does not have

the manic propulsion or single-mindedness of Feydeau nor those extraordinary looping curlicues of verbal absurdity you find in old Ben. What it does have, though, is enormous physical audacity and a sense of characters locked for ever into some strange tic of personality. The naîve, spluttering Tristram, for instance, is a wonderful inversion of normal legal fluency:

> TRISTRAM: Sorry. I've got the contractual finalisations – er – the finalised contractuals – rather, contracts – ready. So there should be no obvious .. er .. er .. er .. oh .. er .. constructions ... er ... obstructions. Right. To the payments and completion. Of it all. (*Pause.*) Yes.
> ROLAND (*after some thought*): Yes, I see. (*He studies Tristram.*) Excuse my asking but you're going into this legal business full time, are you?

Roland's excessive drinking also becomes a prime running gag beautifully embodied by Dinsdale Landen in the Michael Rudman London production as he downed brimming tumblers of Scotch while his eyes widened and his features underwent Etna-like convulsions. Ayckbourn in this play takes the classic rules of farce, bends them, stretches them, teases them into his own particular shape, makes you laugh and also leaves you with a resonant final image: that of Lizzie, like an incapacitated Nora in *A Doll's House*, pausing once more on the threshold both of this Norman mansion and of life itself.

'Suburban Strains' and other musicals

One of the subterranean themes of the farce *Taking Steps* is the difficulty of living up to other people's expectations of oneself. Lizzie, the fugitive wife, complains bitterly to her brother that Roland places her on a pedestal: 'It's a wonderful thing being made to feel like a goddess but after about ten minutes it gets very, very boring. I mean, I daren't do anything normal in front of him now in case it shatters some illusion he's got. I have to leave the room to scratch.' At the time, we laugh. But remarks like that have a habit in Ayckbourn of rebounding (he is a squirrel amongst dramatists, hoarding things away for future use). And, sure enough, when Roland is abandoned by his wife, he remarks to the incoherent solicitor: 'Do you know something interesting? The whole time I've lived with that woman, I have never once seen her scratch herself. Not once. I'd call that unnatural, wouldn't you? Grounds for divorce, don't you think so, Mr Watson? Failure to itch.' Lizzie presents him with an idealised self: he all the time wants the real woman.

Something of this uncertainty about what the other half wants is preserved in Ayckbourn's next project, *Suburban Strains*, a play with music first seen in Scarborough in January 1980 and presented a year later at the Round House in London with, for the first time ever in the metropolis, the original company. This musical, composed by Paul Todd, is about a teacher, Caroline, and switches back and forth between her marriage to a bum actor, whom she finds in bed with one of her pupils, her own subsequent *affaire* with a bullying doctor and her spasms of fretful isolation. It is a delightful show about real people that escapes from most of the recurrent vices of the British musical: sub-Broadway glitziness, the attempt to hack a show out of a recalcitrant novel (often by Dickens, Wells or Bennett) or fey, Slade-school innocence suggesting poisoned *Salad Days*.

But one of the show's real pleasures is the way

Ayckbourn plays tricks with time and space and at the same time touches the nerves of truth. One very good scene is a deft montage of two separate evenings in which Caroline invites two different men in for coffee. One of them is a gourmet bachelor petrified that Caroline will make some untimely sexual advance: the other is a good-looking doctor for whose pass she herself impatiently waits. Out of these wholly credible situations springs a song, 'What Do They Expect?', that applies equally to both of them and that pinpoints a woman's dilemma in not knowing what is expected of her. The same theme could, of course, be applied equally to men in a liberated age when time-honoured courtesies may either be accepted or crushingly repulsed. But Ayckbourn in one song fixes a female problem very perceptively.

Indeed *Suburban Strains* suggests Ayckbourn had learned a lot from his implication in the packaged fiasco of *Jeeves*. Here he allows songs to develop organically from the situation: one very good one, 'Table Talk', uses snatches of bitchy conversation around a dinner-table counterpointed by the heroine's solo reflections. He plays merry hell with conventional time, often contrasting one scene with another to compare Caroline's reactions. He ingeniously uses three concentric stages, of which the inner two can revolve. But, above all, he makes music out of the problems people really face: breaking marriages, periods of adjustment and the determination of lovers to reconstruct the loved one according to their ideal. As Benedict Nightingale wrote:

> All along Caroline has been a natural victim like the put-upon Annie in *The Norman Conquests*. Friends and relations have always patronised, blamed or reviled her, or simply used her adversity as an excuse to talk about

themselves. Now she finds her voice, carriage, breasts, feet, manners and conduct endlessly subjected to her new lover's built-in X-ray machine; and for a moment it looks as if she, like Vera before her, may actually be destroyed by the pressure and the play end where Ayckbourn's work so often has of late, in the dumps.

It does not; and I share something of Mr Nightingale's dismay at a falsely upbeat ending. Caroline, who was freshly and vivaciously played by Lavinia Bertram, discovers her own individuality, which is fine. But, having discovered it, she teams up again with her unemployed actor-husband which is not. At the end, they jointly proclaim: 'Why not settle for today and cuddle up tonight?' I can think of a dozen reasons why not, such as his Humbert Humbert-like passion for teenage girls and her new-found discovery of her true self. It is a much softer ending than Ayckbourn would have permitted in a play. But it is the one decisive blot on a civilised musical about genuine emotional problems.

Ayckbourn's fascination with the possibilities of musical theatre continued in 1980 with two lunch-time musical revues, *First Course* and *Second Helping*. And in July 1981 he and Paul Todd came up with three linked, 50-minute lunchtime musicals, *Me, Myself and I* (which were presented by the Orange Tree, Richmond in December 1982 as a consecutive evening's entertainment). They are a further development in that they show Ayckbourn applying to the musical the kind of technical ingenuity he had used in his plays while also continuing to show women attempting to escape from identities other people construct for them.

The protagonist is Mary Yately – 'aged thirty-four, no A-Levels, four children' – about to be interviewed by the

Alan Ayckbourn

Evening Echo as a winner of their Mum of the Year competition which she did not even go in for. But Ayckbourn's initial conceit is to have Mary played and sung by three different actresses representing the tripartite nature of her personality. There is the Ego of the frustrated suburban housewife, the Superego who is a cool, eyebrow-shrugging worldling and the Id who is a provocative and raging sensualist. As a technical device it is extremely adroit because (rather as in Peter Nichols's *Passion Play*) it enables one-third of Mary to look on in astonishment or even horror at what her alter egos are up to. But it is also a way of commenting on the complex, triple-decker nature of Mary's personality: after years of cooking, cleaning and washing for six, Mary is able to release her long-suppressed desires.

This also enables Ayckbourn as lyricist and Paul Todd as composer to write in a wide variety of musical styles. 'Open for Love' is an exuberant, pastiche-Dietrich torch-song in which the all-seeing I wraps herself lasciviously round the surprised reporter. The 'Wife-Swapping Dance' is a jolly medieval roundelay about the key-in-the-ring sexual romping that goes on in suburban housing estates. And 'Teaching the Children to Speak' is a laconic nursery-time fable about the horrors of being stuck all day with Janet-and-John books – though the husband's alleged presence in South Martinique owes more to the rhyming dictionary than to plausibility.

Once again the ending may strike some as sentimental with husband and wife agreeing to 'give it another go' after Mary's competition-winning has been exploded as pure fantasy. But, as Robin Thornber pointed out, this is cunningly counter-poised against the theme that you never get a second chance which gives the assumed reconciliation a tart sting. It is also heartening to find a musical in which means and ends are in such close harmony. It is a deliberately small-scale show; but yet it says something true about the bubbling inner-lives of women apparently clamped and suffocated by domestic routine.

Successful on a small scale with *Me, Myself and I*, the Ayckbourn–Todd musical combination came in for something of a drubbing with their next show, *Making Tracks*, which enjoyed some success at Scarborough in March 1982 but which got a lot of critical flak at Greenwich Theatre in March 1983. Sheridan Morley in *Punch* called it 'deeply disappointing'. Clive Hirschhorn in the *Sunday Express* rated it 'a disaster'. Only John Barber in the *Daily Telegraph* expressed lukewarm approval, describing it as 'an endearing show of no great pretensions'. Yet seeing it late in its run, I found a packed house obviously having a good night out and displaying unstinted enthusiasm at the end. By the standards of Ayckbourn's own best tragi-comedies, the show was well short of a masterpiece; yet it was not quite the resounding stinker many critics suggested.

Making Tracks is unusual in being set in a tatty recording studio (Pete Atkin's *A and R*, presented by the RSC in 1978, was the only previous musical to use that setting). The plot revolves around the crisis facing Stan Hackett, a third-rate impresario and ex-songwriter. Part-owner of the studios, he is in debt for eight grand to a menacing loan-shark, Wolfe Devine. Stan has arranged to make a demo-disc on Sunday with a singer, Sandy Beige, whom he has spotted in his cups at a local ballroom. And he has until four o'clock that Sunday afternoon (when the drummer has to go off for a celebratory birthday tea for his dead father) to come up with a hit single. If he does not, Wolfe will bring in the heavy mob.

As dramatist, lyricist and director, Ayckbourn

ingeniously exploits the possibilities of the recording-studio setting (well realised in Michael Holt's design). On the upper level is a control cubicle: on the lower level the studio. Each is separated from the other in terms of sound: a point made in the opening moments when the pseudonymous Sandy enters the cubicle and tries to attract the attention of the engineer in the studio by pressing her hand against an invisible wall of glass. So the audience, throughout the play, hears what it hears, from the control cubicle's point of view. Sometimes the studio is a hive of activity but totally inaudible. At other times, when the studio microphones are live, we hear people when they are close to the mike and see them mouthing away like goldfish when they are not. Ayckbourn even has actors coming into microphone-range in the middle of a word.

As an ex-radio producer, Ayckbourn knows all about the deathtrap potential of studio technology (anyone who has worked in radio knows how private conversations can be suddenly picked up by a live microphone). He also remembers *Singin' In The Rain*. Towards the climax of *Making Tracks*, Stan is making a last-ditch attempt to put together his hit single with the ludicrously unmusical Sandy Beige mouthing away into a deliberately dead microphone while Lace – Wolfe Devine's current moll and, as it happens, Stan's singing ex-wife – is doing the real recording, surreptitiously crouching in a phone booth with a head-set. Wolfe, the heavy, surveys the studio scene approvingly, blithely unaware that his girl friend is doing the actual singing. Until, of course, the fatal moment comes when Sandy walks away from the microphone to query something and the singing miraculously continues. It is a good gag; and none the worse for being an echo of that famous moment in *Singin' In The Rain* when Jean Hagen's dumb blonde is miming away on stage and the curtains behind her part to reveal Debbie Reynolds supplying the actual vocals. Ayckbourn, as usual, even builds on the joke by having the phone ring in the booth at the same time as the main deception is revealed.

But Ayckbourn does not simply use the recording studio for comic effect. The musical numbers also deploy its possibilities. Thus the technical wizardry of Rog, the recording engineer (a shy guy nursing a secret passion for Sandy Beige) is shown in a number called 'Alright for Level' in which he brings up and fades out the drummer, the keyboard players and the guitarist before mixing them in perfect unison while reminding us:

> God's an engineer.
> A balanced universe –
> God, it's got to be
> Made by an engineer.

In the climactic number to the first half, 'Words And Music', Ayckbourn and Todd not only parody a vast range of musical styles from Doris Day to Bob Marley: Ayckbourn also has one character, Stan, leaping around between the control cubicle and the recording studio. And another number, 'Recording You', makes full use of the verbal and musical possibilities of words like recording, replaying and receiving: two couples, in fact, express their intertwined emotional states via the technology of the studio with Rog, for instance, expressing his private feelings about Sandy in the cubicle and his public ones through the talkback system.

With all this in its favour, why is *Making Tracks* something less than a total success? Part of the problem is that the dramatic situation itself is somewhat static. We know from the beginning there is a crisis. Will Stan save himself from the menacing heavy and keep the Wolfe at the door? Will he overcome the fact that his trumpeted discovery, Sandy, cannot really sing? We also know that, in the end, it will all be resolved. Indeed, as soon as we discover that Lace herself is a onetime professional singer, it does not take much guessing how it will all work out. But the predestined end seems rather a long time coming; and one is reminded that all good musicals need a second idea – a sub-plot, if you like - to sustain them. In *My Fair Lady*, to take an obvious example, we do not simply want to know whether Higgins will pass Eliza off as a Duchess - we also want to know whether she will marry or settle down with the rebarbative Professor. Here the mild love interest between Rog and Sandy is not enough to quicken our pulses.

Paul Todd's numbers, though musically varied and stylish, also seem to hold up the action rather than advance it. One feels Ayckbourn has come up with a dramatic idea and Paul Todd has supplied the musical illustration to it. But I would not pillory them for trying; nor would I attack them for seeking to escape from the stereotypical British musical in which tunes are simply tacked on to a respected literary source. The problem here is that the dramatic crisis seems both elongated and slightly improbable (would a practised showman like Stan, even in his cups, have put his money on a palpable no-no like Sandy?) and that not even Mr Todd's nine songs can quite disguise that fact. Technically, *Making Tracks* is an interesting experiment; it simply suggests that the Ayckbourn–Todd combination needs a bit more time in the workshop before it achieves the seamless, inevitable conjunction of words and music, narrative idea and numbers.

'Season's Greetings'

To me *Season's Greetings* (first seen in Scarborough in September 1980, at the Roundhouse, London, in December of the same year and, in a revised version at Greenwich Theatre and the Apollo in 1982) is something of a test-case. Those who regard Ayckbourn as no more than a deft Scarborough *farceur* will perceive in it no more than a jolly night out. But anyone who regards Ayckbourn as a master of mood and situation, a dramatist who can balance what Harold Hobson called 'ineradicable sadness' with present laughter, will see in it his most Chekhovian play. Of course, the comparison is flattering: Ayckbourn's characters do not have the memory-penetrating resonance of Chekhov's. But Ayckbourn does here show the great Russian dramatist's ability to mix laughter and tears and to keep you swinging between the two like a pendulum.

The setting (as in *Absurd Person Singular*) is once again Christmas: the perfect season for Ayckbourn since, as someone said, it is the time when we make whoopee and commit suicide and when families come together in an often-doomed attempt at festivity. With the rather aptly-named Neville and Belinda Bunker, merriment and disaster converge. They themselves, after eight years of marriage, are going through familiar stresses: that is to say, he constantly retreats to his workshop and tinkers endlessly with machinery while she hungers for life, excitement and human contact. The other Yule celebrants are not much happier: Belinda's sister, Phyllis, is a childless dipso who can turn the preparation of dinner into an orgy of blood and flour and who is married to a self-confessed failure of a doctor with a passion for puppet-plays that bore the pants off kids. Harvey Bunker, Neville's uncle, is a gun-toting ex-security guard with apocalyptic visions of street violence. Neville's ex-partner, Eddie, is a bovine boor with a child-harassed wife. But the real catalyst among the pigeons is Clive, a divorced novelist who is the Christmas guest of Belinda's sexless sister, Rachel, and who in the course of festivities, triggers Belinda's lust and Harvey's violence. Christmas, *chez* Bunker, is a horribly typical English mix of rows, tears, booze, sex and television.

A cynic might say that Ayckbourn is whipping up the play out of stock ingredients; and it is true that some of the characters and situations do carry not-too-distant echoes. It is not merely the Christmas setting. Both the sibling sexual rivalry and the Fascist elder convinced England is on the verge of breakdown were present in *Sisterly Feelings*; the husband whose heart is in his toolshed takes us back to *Just Between Ourselves*; and the bubbling marital crisis might be said to be Ayckbourn *passim*. Yet I believe *Season's Greetings* is original and different in that it pushes the element of banked-up frustration (both sexual and psychopathic) further than ever before and in that it achieves the perfect synthesis of comedy and tragedy, laughter and despair.

Ayckbourn's mastery of situation is not something imposed: it grows out of a whole treasure trail of carefully planted incidents. Thus he makes it clear that when Belinda first claps eyes on novelist Clive it is sex at first sight: her marital misery coincides with his intuitive sympathy. But the consummation devoutly to be wished cannot happen straight off. Ayckbourn is also planting clues about husband Neville's do-it-yourself wizardry with a Christmas tree that lights up and bursts into song at the press of a remote-control button, about Harvey's sinister present of an alarm clock that sounds like a firebell and of the drunken Phyllis's gift of a clockwork drumming-bear. These tricks and treats are each indications of the donor's character: they are also carefully stored away under the Christmas tree. So when Belinda and Clive feverishly go to it in the hallway (because, plausibly, she refuses to make love in her living room and kitchen) late at night under the self-same tree, their lust quite literally triggers off all these mechanical devices. Two people copulating under a Christmas tree is not inherently funny: it is only funny because of who they are and because the ground has been so thoroughly prepared. The only parallel for this kind of long-term comic strategy is the brilliant scene in Feydeau's *Le Dindon* where warning-bells secreted under a hotel mattress go off not when the bed is occupied by a pair of adulterers but by an innocent military doctor and his stone-deaf wife. Comedy of this kind is always about preparation and thrift; and Ayckbourn is thrifty as they come.

But his Chekhovian ability to fuse contradictory emotions (possibly the highest delight the theatre has to offer) is seen best in his treatment of the hapless doctor, Bernard, and the ex-security guard, Harvey. Throughout the first act the prospect of Bernard's epic Boxing Day puppet-show is a running gag: snide comments are passed about last year's *Ali Baba* where the forty thieves came on with ten-minute intervals between them and this year there is an understandable nervousness about *The Three Little Pigs* ('Just the three of them is it?' enquires Neville). And when, in the second act, Bernard previews his wooden epic everything goes predictably awry. Under pressure, Bernard himself turns from a mild-mannered no-hoper into a petty tyrant juggling with cardboard scenery, stuffed pigs and recalcitrant helpers like Eddie's wife who keeps knocking things over with her child-bearing belly. Theatrical chaos, even on a miniaturised scale, is always funny and we guiltlessly laugh. But when the jeering Harvey brings things to a climax by hurling the wolf in the air, crashing the puppets together and kicking over the scenery, our laughter is suddenly stilled. Bernard's riposte also makes us ashamed of our participation in Harvey's abuse:

> BERNARD: You are a loathsome man, Harvey, you really are. You're almost totally negative, do you know that? And that's such an easy thing to be, isn't it? So long as you stay negative, you're absolutely safe from laughter or criticism because you've never made anything or done anything that people can criticize. All they can really say about you is that you're a snob, a bigot, a racist, a chauvinist, an ignorant, insensitive, narrow-minded, intolerant, humourless wart.
>
> HARVEY (*having digested this*): Very well. We shall see. We'll see who's negative. Ha. . . . We'll see. (*Speaking to the house in general.*) You'll all be glad of me sometime. Laugh now but you'll see.

This is high theatrical craft for a variety of reasons. One is that our implicit mockery of Bernard suddenly swings round to sympathy. Another is that his outburst, however surprising, grows out of his tenacious character ('He's sacrificed his whole career to try and cure me', says his wife in the previous scene). And a third is that it directly affects the action of the play in that Harvey's Vanya-like urge to be remembered bears fruit in the next dawn-scene when he determines to nab Clive whom he wildly suspects of being a homosexual looter. I have frequently in this book called Ayckbourn a master of situation; but the real sign of artistry in a playwright is when character and situation merge imperceptibly so that what people do and what they are become indistinguishable. That is what happens here.

Onwards and Upwards

Something even harder to convey is Ayckbourn's feeling for theatrical poetry. Eric Bentley once drew a crucial distinction between poetry *in* the theatre and poetry *of* the theatre: the former consists of iambic pentameters, alexandrines or whatever whereas the latter can arise from something as simple as the placement of characters on a stage at a particular moment in time. In Peter Stein's Berlin production of Gorki's *Summerfolk* there was a heart-stopping poetic moment when a group of characters walked through a wood at dusk after a picnic. Such effects can also be achieved aurally as well as visually: the climax to *The Cherry Orchard* when the house has finally emptied, the doors have all been locked and the axe starts to swing at the trees rarely fails to take one's breath away. Again, keeping due proportion, one has to say that Ayckbourn knows how to achieve just such effects. When the lonely thirty-eight-year-old spinster, Rachel, whose secretly longed-for sexual relationships invariably turn out platonic, talks about her plight with Clive we are inevitably moved. But no words she utters are as theatrically moving as the image that confronts us in the final scene of the first act. It is Christmas night. Everyone is slightly drunk. In the dining room a noisy, tipsy game of Snakes and Ladders proceeds apace. But, in the darkened sitting room, the canned Eddie sits there with mouth agape while Rachel sits alone and still in a window-seat quietly nursing her drink. That is pure theatre because it distils a mood: Rachel knows she has lost Clive to her sexually-exuberant sister and has quietly withdrawn both from Christmas games and, in the end, from a segment of life itself.

John Barber got it right when, in reviewing this play, he wrote of the way it demonstrates that 'it is not the big events that age and kill us: it is the way people look away and say nothing and run up the stairs in tears'. By setting much of the action in a hallway – though he makes us constantly aware of what people are up to in the dining room and living room – Ayckbourn makes the most of those possibilities. People are forever coming, going, crossing, barging upstairs or downstairs and the way they do it is always indicative of some shift in mood. Bernard making dogged journeys through the hall with his cumbersome puppet theatre; Pattie shouting from the stairway to Eddie to come and say goodnight to the children; Rachel standing in the hallway at dawn the day after Boxing Day ready to transport her writer-chum to the station – all these and many more moments bear out Barber's point that in Ayckbourn life is made up of myriad tiny crises.

I have heard the objection made to the play that you never glimpse the children, who are the focal point of any family Christmas. But even if the kids are not seen or heard, their presence is invariably felt: they are potent off-stage characters like Dick and Lottie Potter. And the real point is that these Ayckbourn adults themselves bear the sticky imprint of childhood: not merely in the way they purloin the kids' comic books and play their board games but in the way they squabble over prize possessions (like Belinda and Rachel), retreat into their secret world (like Neville) or nurse false hopes (like the deluded Eddie who believes he is to become branch-manager of one of Neville's stores). Christmas is a time for children: it is also, Ayckbourn implies in this harshly witty play, a time when adults regress, exposing their wants, fears, needs and frustrations in a manner hushed up at other seasons.

'Way Upstream'

'She's as headstrong as an allegory on the banks of the

Nile', remarked Mrs Malaprop of the heroine of *The Rivals*. What we have in *Way Upstream* (first seen at Scarborough in September 1981 and then at the Lyttelton in October 1982) is an allegory set between the banks of the River Orb. In every sense the play marks a radical departure for Ayckbourn in that it is, in his own words, 'a fable about evil' and a comment on the state of the nation. It also breaks new ground, almost literally, in that the action is set on a four-berth cabin-cruiser on a seven-day journey from Hadforth Boat Yard to Armageddon Bridge and beyond. If it is not a total triumph, it is also not the spectacular disaster that many eagerly anticipated when the play had its much-postponed London first night at the Lyttelton in October 1982. As Benedict Nightingale said, 'it's surely inspiring to find our leading comic dramatist insisting on improbable new challenges for himself'.

One problem lies in disentangling the play from the hazards involved in mounting it. Even on the smaller scale of Scarborough, the flooding of the auditorium involved technical difficulties and the cancellation of a preview. At the Lyttelton the problems got predictably bigger. A fibreglass tank, made from 24 pieces, weighing 1¼ tons when empty and finally containing 6000 gallons of murky Thames water, got damaged by the continual movement of being taken on and off stage. On top of that, three stage technicians hidden inside the cabin-cruiser had severe communication problems because of the perils of passing live electric wires through 3ft 6in of water. Preview performances were cancelled. The play's budget shot up from £25,000 to £40,000 because of repairs and delays. A disaster was bruited. When it was finally unveiled, the play got interestingly mixed reviews and the theatre was packed with audiences drawn by the promise of something startlingly different.

Put all that aside and one finds (on the page) a very well-knit, logically constructed play. It starts, lightly and funnily, with two couples setting out on a river-cruise holiday. They are Keith, a tinpot industrialist who owns a Novelty Toy firm, and his shrewish ex-showgirl wife, June; Alistair, his amiable, ineffectual business partner, and his nervous, unflamboyant wife Emma. From the start, Ayckbourn hoists warning signals that the voyage is not going to be exactly smooth. Keith's train has been derailed; the boat originally chosen has suffered engine failure; there is trouble with the workers back at the factory; Keith and June are in the midst of a marital crack-up; and the ultimate destination is Armageddon Bridge. But, for all this, Ayckbourn gets a lot of comedy out of landlubber Keith's determination to be captain and to pose as a blazered Bligh with the help of a book called *River Cruising on the Orb*. It is a perfectly plausible account of an ominous upriver trip backed up by occasional reminders that: 'Boats are a society in miniature. Everyone has a role, everyone has a function.' And the daily arrival alongside of Keith's secretary, Mrs Hatfield, with news of deepening industrial unrest is a reminder that when the English go on holiday they still take the work-ethic with them.

The tone subtly changes with the arrival of Vince, a vagrant river-person claiming to be a 'victim of the system', who helps get the boat afloat after Alistair has managed to run it aground. At first, Vince seems a charming bum with an eye for the willing June. But soon he is imposing a rigid discipline on the crew and even renaming the parts of the boat to gain control. He then brings along an uninvited aristo, bird-watching girl friend, Fleur, deposes Keith as skipper with the connivance of the women, introduces sexually exotic night-games, maroons the hapless Alistair on an island and forces his non-swimming wife Emma to walk the plank. Vince becomes the fascist-spirit in action. But finally Alistair, who has so far stood helplessly by, contrives to maim Vince and abandon him in the company of Fleur and June. He and Emma sail the boat past Armageddon Bridge and, pursued by the retributive cries of the abandoned trio plus Keith and Mrs Hatfield, they take off their clothes and jump into the water in a defiant gesture of liberation.

Clearly the cabin-cruiser and its crew are a metaphor for modern England. Vince represents Fascism, Fleur aristocratic decadence, Keith capitalist arrogance, June sensuous passivity and Alistair and Emma all the quiet, moderate, reasonable people whose voices scarcely ever get heard. Ayckbourn himself does nothing to dispel this interpretation with talk of 'the final collapse of civilisation as we know it' and Alistair himself conceding that they will have to make the hazardous journey back through enemy territory even though it is filled with unreasonable people. 'Then we reasonable people', he says, 'will just have to go back and reason with them.' The play is, quite specifically, a plea for moderation in an ugly, extremist world where petty tyrannies of the right and left are, in Ayckbourn's view, increasingly rampant.

In a fascinating Radio 3 feature about the play's first production, *Various Stages*, Ayckbourn described to Ronald Hayman the play's origins:

Things are happening in the world which are quite impossible to ignore even for a writer living in Scarborough and writing plays ostensibly for entertainment. Certain things occurred to me about life and people's attitude to it and the world and all that and it made me want to write a play about responsibility and

159

where it lay. I suppose in a way it's a play about people like me who tend to avoid such things. I'm totally apolitical. At the same time one is aware that if you sit around letting it all happen people get elected you don't like very much and you've only yourself to blame for not having taken part. . . . But it was the introduction of two extra characters that made the difference. There's this jolly little boatload of well-cushioned, middle-class people jogging along upstream on a river. All Vince and Fleur do is exploit the weaknesses in that and bring them down. They exploit the weaknesses in Keith and June who are already cracked people and just splinter. They expose weaknesses in Alistair and Emma and all but bring them down. In fact, what makes it a comedy rather than a tragedy is that Alistair and Emma rally rather sheepishly and Britishly. They actually win if only to fight another battle. In that sense it's a fable. It's a fable about evil. The two outside characters are as evil as anyone has ever written: what makes it more fabulous is that there is no attempt to justify their reaction. They are simply filled with a sense of what I think the world is full of at the moment, a nebulous hate.

In writing a state-of-the-nation play Ayckbourn was pursuing an honourable theatrical tradition: Shaw's *Heartbreak House*, Priestley's *Bees on the Boatdeck* (where a boat specifically symbolises England, civilisation and decency), Osborne's *The Entertainer*, Nichols's *The National Health*, Brenton and Hare's *Brassneck* are just some of the many plays that take the moral temperature of England. I see no reason why Ayckbourn should be attacked for doing the same. The one real argument against his play is that, at least in Ayckbourn's own epic-scale National production, the means seemed disproportionate to the ends. The endless spinning and turning of the cabin-cruiser, the onset of a real rainstorm, the lowering of Armageddon Bridge from the flies all gave the play a visual rhetoric that seemed excessive for a study of the 'nebulous hate' abroad in the land. When read, the play seems like a carefully graded account of the way daemonic extremism gradually makes itself manifest: in production, it began to seem like *The Four Horsemen of the Apocalypse* crossed with a watery *Ben Hur*. In short, Ayckbourn the writer was not all that well served by Ayckbourn the director.

That said, the play does have a lot going for it: not least Ayckbourn's ability to reveal character through action, to show what people are through what they do. One of the play's funniest scenes has Keith and the rest bunglingly attempting to moor the craft while behind them the alleged camaraderie of the river turns to angry, intemperate hooting. Keith bullies and blusters, shouting at everyone including the unfortunate Mrs Hatfield on the bank (KEITH: 'Bollard. Use your bollard.' MRS HATFIELD: 'I don't have a bollard.'). June complains that it's like being in hell. Alistair throws the bow line into the water. Emma, commanded to take the helm, more by luck than judgement nudges the boat in towards the shore. As a piece of theatre, it is a desperately funny image of marine chaos; and, as a metaphor, it is a reminder of the hectoring incompetence of the managerial classes.

Equally the scene where Vince takes over command of the boat and its crew (while Keith is out of sight having a shower) is very dexterous theatre. It reminds us that the way to power lies through language as much as brute force: relying on the ignorance of the landlubbers (and the fact that he has thrown the handbook overboard), Vince proceeds to rename all the parts of the boat to the utter confusion of the crew:

This area here, the so-called cockpit, is in fact your kedge deck. Further astern, stepping on to the roof of the poop cabin – below me is called the poop cabin – this deck area here is called the dodger. And here, right at the very stern, this area we call the snuffle deck. For obvious reasons. Finally, that narrow corridor running from your snuffle down each side of your dodger, round your kedge, forward again past your weevil and meeting at your gaff are your port and starboard squeezes.

This is the theatrical equivalent of that marvellous Henry Reed poem, *Naming of Parts* ('This is the lower sling swivel. And this is the upper sling swivel, whose use you will see when you are given your slings') except that Vince's blend of sense and nonsense is an instrument of personal power: a way of achieving dominance through assumed technical mastery. What again contributes to Ayckbourn's political message is that June, Emma and, to a lesser extent, Alistair all succumb to Vince's menacing magnetism.

Also significant, as Ayckbourn himself implies, is that Vince's tactics work only because everyone else is fractious, divided and weak. They are divided: he rules. Keith and June are deftly established as a couple whose marriage is held together by an about-to-snap thread. Even Emma is disappointed that the man she has married is not a hero or leader but a tame, submissive wimp. In one of the play's cruellest and most effective moments, Fleur chats up Alistair who is mooching alone on the bank while everyone else is having a party in the saloon. She even tempts the reluctant Alistair into a dance only to reveal that Emma has bet her a pound that she cannot get him to do a little wistful shuffle. It is a small scene in terms of the play's overall gesture; yet it is indicative of the way even a good woman like Emma is instinctively drawn to the side of the strong and powerful.

The play has its weak spots. Alistair's transformation from hyper-helpless chump to scourge-of-evil is a little too drastic to be convincing. Vince's motiveless malignity is a little bit hard to fathom: Ayckbourn, I suspect, is more at ease with daily acts of domestic cruelty than with wholesale piratical evil. Indeed, one wishes Ayckbourn could have been a little more specific about the 'nebulous hate' he feels present in British society. What exactly is its source? Or indeed its manifestation? Fascist rallies? Left-wing intolerance? Delinquent youth? Crabbed middle-aged hangers and floggers? If we are getting ever closer to Armageddon Bridge, who exactly is taking us there?

Yet, when one has notched up one's reservations, it still strikes me as heartening that a writer famous for his resonant domestic comedies, farces, tragi-comedies and indeed tragi-farces should strike out once more in a new direction. When dramatists plough the same furrow, we carp and bitch. Yet when they also expand their frontiers and, as in Ayckbourn's case, venture into the field of political allegory, we also reach for our hatchets. To me *Way Upstream*, for all its National Theatre magnification, proves that Ayckbourn is a real theatrical artist: reluctant to stand still and always trying to push the frontiers of drama further outwards.

7

The State of the Nation

My conviction that Ayckbourn has the capacity for development of the true artist has been borne out by the events of the Eighties. At a time of life when other dramatists start to rest on their laurels, count their winnings or retire to Shropshire to pen disgruntled autobiographies, he has not only carried on writing but also broadened his canvas and refined his technique. The popular view is that he started as a boulevard lightweight and has since gone on to write increasingly dark and sombre plays. But there is more to it than that. I would say that he began as a ruthless and unsparing observer of sexual politics and middle-class manners. Now his subject is, more often than not, the state of the nation and the decline of our culture.

What is fascinating about Ayckbourn today is that he shows an ungovernable concern with the quality of British life: in particular, the prevailing moral, ethical and religious vacuum. The turning-point was obviously *Way Upstream* with its call to the shy, the sheepish and the non-committed to stand up to evil and to protect basic decencies. Since then Ayckbourn has written a number of plays just as much concerned with taking the moral temperature of the nation. *Woman In Mind* (1985) is not only about an emotionally neglected middle-aged woman's descent into madness but also about the failure of orthodox Christian morality to cope with individual unhappiness. *A Small Family Business* (1987) is as much a political play as Caryl Churchill's *Serious Money*: its very title invokes the entrepreneurial values we are all supposed to endorse and the action shows that those who make them their god end up endorsing theft, drug-trafficking and murder. In the futuristic *Henceforward* (1987) Ayckbourn posits a world where law and order have broken down and where people live in computerised bunkers enslaved by the very machines they have created. And in *Man of the Moment* (1988) he suggests we live in a world where the criminal is accorded heroic status, where his victim is regarded as a bit of a mug and where television offers daily distortions of reality.

Ayckbourn has become a much more pronounced moralist without sacrificing his capacity as an entertainer: his plays, with the exception of *A Small Family Business*, still get premiered in Scarborough where seaside audiences arrive looking for a good night out. As director of a theatre primarily devoted to new writing, he recently gave me a capsule definition of his whole philosophy: 'The brief I give writers is the one I was originally given by Stephen Joseph: by all means write what you want but for God's sake say it in a way that is going to appeal to people who come to the theatre. I think we encourage a healthy commercialism in the writer. In the end we say that if your message is an empty theatre it is useless. Let's see how clever we can be at saying unpalatable things in a palatable manner.'

Alan Ayckbourn

Saying harsh things in a beguiling manner has long been Ayckbourn's forté. But he has now become so technically adroit that he can combine farce and tragedy in a single moment and leave an audience caught in a turmoil of laughter and horror (something Chekhov did to perfection in *Uncle Vanya* where the hero's attempt to shoot the Professor is both ridiculously comic and a symptom of his desperation). This is partly because his plays are finely-tuned instruments which he directs with zealous care. But the world has come to realise in the late Eighties something which Scarborough has long known: that Ayckbourn is a very fine director of other people's work as well as his own.

From September 1986 to March 1988 Ayckbourn took a sabbatical from Scarborough and formed his own autonomous company under the generous umbrella of Peter Hall's National Theatre. For many people the result was a revelation. Ayckbourn began his tenure with a revival of the very first Aldwych farce, *Tons of Money*, chiefly memorable for Michael Gambon's performance as the butler Sprules, who became a domestic Quasimodo with thin strands of black hair plastered across the dome of his head like the kind of inky squiggles children make over an egg. Ayckbourn followed that with a sensational production of *A View From The Bridge*, again with Michael Gambon. Arthur Miller declared it the best version of the play he had ever seen. What was remarkable was the way the tragedy grew out of a beautifully realised domestic and social context. The way Gambon's Eddie Carbone flung himself into his chair or expected his niece to tug off his boots told you everything about this man's bullying patriarchal status: equally, the kids playing on the stoop and the looming presence of Brooklyn Bridge reminded you of the surrounding community whose laws he was to violate. Conversely, Ayckbourn's own production of *A Small Family Business* became the tragedy of a man who succumbs to, rather than flagrantly attacks, the communal ethic. Only Ayckbourn's production of John Ford's incest-drama, *'Tis Pity She's A Whore*, disappointed largely because the two main roles were undercast and because, as Ayckbourn himself admits, he had no time to teach them the basic rules of verse-speaking.

But Ayckbourn's metropolitan success as a director has added to the complexity of his life. He is committed to running the Stephen Joseph Theatre in Scarborough, while transferring productions such as *Man of the Moment* to the West End. Ayckbourn has emerged in the late Eighties as our most complete man of the theatre: a writer, director and producer of boundless fertility. But in tracing his development during the decade one must begin with a work that both in its sheer scale and in its demands on its leading players has no exact precedent in the history of drama.

'Intimate Exchanges'

You leave a cinema but forget your raincoat. You go back and find in the next seat your future wife. Alan Ayckbourn once gave critic John Barber that example of the way our lives are governed by chance: the way a single moment may determine the whole pattern of our existence. It is an idea he pursues to its ultimate conclusion in *Intimate Exchanges*: a cycle of eight separate plays that present the characters with different choices leading to a totality of sixteen different versions comprising, in all, thirty-one scenes. Add to that the fact it is written for two actors and you have some idea of its complexity. As Martin

Hoyle wrote in the *Financial Times*, it is rather as if Priestley's *Dangerous Corner* had been rewritten by a comic computer; and when the plays had their first London staging at Greenwich Theatre in the summer of 1984, I remember audiences standing in front of a complex diagram in the foyer, charting the various permutations, in a state of dazed bewilderment. But the first point to make about this wildly experimental project is that it could only have been undertaken by a writer running his own theatre who knew exactly what talents were available: a point Ayckbourn made in an interview with Paul Allen in *Marxism Today*.

'When this company had done its last performance of *Way Upstream* in Houston in America, most of the company were so exhausted that they all wanted a rest, except Lavinia Bertram and Robin Herford who were quite happy to carry on. It came to me that here was an opportunity, without putting anybody out of work, to do my two-hander that I'd always wanted to do. Here were two actors I'd worked with for years and years, two people who would actually trust me, and I could trust them to do a play of an enormous nature. *Sisterly Feelings* was a play in which there were alternative scenes in the middle but this was a small-scale version of what I really wanted to do, which was a play that developed from one tiny little moment – whether a woman decides to smoke a cigarette or not – into two separate scenes, four choices of third scene, eight choices of fourth and sixteen choices of fifth scene. To do that hair-raising amount of material and to ask two people to do it, to learn the equivalent of half the Bible, required an enormous amount of faith. If I'd carried that around the West End in a suitcase, which is what the scripts would have needed, I don't think anybody would necessarily have bought it.'

The State of the Nation

The question is: does *Intimate Exchanges* work? I would say 'Yes' and 'No'. The scheme is highly ambitious. The plays contain some of Ayckbourn's most brilliant writing. The practical problem is that you have to see or read all eight plays, with their multiple variations, to grasp the full complexity of what Ayckbourn is saying and in the real world that rarely happens. The plays were given with their original cast in Scarborough, Greenwich and for a season at the Ambassadors in London. They have since been seen in Toronto. But the tendency has been for regional companies to pick out the one play they prefer. The truth is you need to see all the plays to understand what Ayckbourn is driving at.

If he had taken up twenty hours of stage-time simply to prove that our lives are governed by chance, the work would be mechanical and repetitive. What Ayckbourn is actually saying is something much more complicated: that a momentary decision or a chance event may overturn our lives but that our destiny is also determined by character. In some plays the emphasis is on the fortuitous: in others people's lives remain obstinately untransformed because of who they are. *In toto*, the plays are about the contradictoriness of human existence and the casual way in which we often destroy those to whom we are closest.

But the whimsicality of chance and the mystery of human character are the twin ideas around which all the plays revolve. The operation of the former is seen at its most direct in the one that opens the cycle, *Affairs in a Tent*. Like all the others, it is set in and around Bilbury Lodge Preparatory School. Like all the others, it starts with Celia – the frustrated, menopausal wife of the school's headmaster Toby – deciding whether or not to have a cigarette (it may give smokers cause for cheer that in the four plays where she decides to have her first puff of the day she is a much nicer person than in the four where she disdains the weed). Like all the others, it spans a period of five years and ends in a churchyard.

As so often in Ayckbourn, the action springs from marital discontent and female frustration. Celia, who once worked for a firm that organised conferences, is trapped in a stale, pointless marriage to the alcoholic Toby who seethes with rage towards the world at large and who communicates with his wife largely through insult. So when Lionel Hepplewick, the school caretaker, comes to lay some crazy paving in Celia's garden and reveals himself to be a man of some sensitivity (who prefers Bruckner to Mahler) and ambition, it is not surprising that Celia responds to him both physically and intellectually. Here is a man of unrealised potential, like herself, who turns out to be a master baker ('A what?' Celia inquires, thinking she has misheard). Celia, in fit of slightly hysterical excitement, gets carried away by the idea of the two of them going into partnership and running their own bakery business.

At the end of the third scene a choice confronts Celia. Either she repents of her sudden rush of blood to the head, confesses all to her husband and tries to shake off the determined Lionel, or she tells Toby that she is going to leave him for a while to start up a new business venture. The latter choice leads into the central scene that gives the play its title. It is a piece of vintage Ayckbourn in that it starts as panic-stricken farce and ends with the total crack-up of the desperate heroine. The setting is a tea-tent during the School Sports Day where an overtaxed Celia is trying to cater for the VIPs with the help of nothing more than an iron-hard, monstrously inedible loaf baked by the ludicrously incompetent Lionel. It is a painful scene which climaxes in Celia presiding over an imaginary doll's tea-party and being wrapped up in a cloth by Miles, the Chairman of the Governors, and bundled under the table.

At this point we really do see how Ayckbourn's law of chance operates. In one scenario Toby, Celia's husband, enters to console his mummified wife and to promise to look after her always. That leads on to a final scene five years later in which Celia is a permanent invalid being looked after by a cossetting Toby while the hopeless Lionel has gone on to run a thriving fast-food joint known as Kwickieburgers. The other scenario has Lionel come in to rescue the trussed-up Celia who bites him in the leg for his pains and clings on to him for grim death. That leads to a final scene in which Celia is a high-powered executive with a luxury-food business, Lionel is her obeisant chauffeur and Toby is ekeing out his days in wretched solitude.

Clearly Ayckbourn is saying that chance is vital. If Toby discovers Celia during her tea-tent breakdown, she is doomed to a life of catatonic misery (one is reminded of Vera at the end of *Just Between Ourselves*). If Lionel discovers her, she eventually fulfils her potential but also sacrifices something of her humanity. Ayckbourn dramatises chance very skilfully. But in order to make his point he presents us with rather stark choices: Celia as pathetic wreck or Celia as bustling New Woman. And if Lionel is such a hopeless klutz who can't even bake a decent loaf or tend the school boiler without blowing it up, you rather wonder how he manages to turn into a successful entrepreneur. I am reminded, oddly enough, of *Romeo and Juliet* where Shakespeare undermines his own thesis that human affairs are governed by luck (or fate) by creating characters of such vividness that you feel they would transcend fortune. Although this play is very funny, Ayckbourn never quite solves this central problem; you feel that Celia and Lionel, particularly, are imagined in such depth that their lives would be determined by something more than the arbitrariness of chance.

But, as the plays go on, they become increasingly rich. The characters acquire a novelistic density. The settings become ever more varied: one play revolves round a cricket match, another round a game of golf. What also happens is that Ayckbourn, like all good dramatists, starts to question and subvert his own thesis about the governing power of chance. By the time we get to the seventh play, *A One Man Protest*, Ayckbourn not only achieves a perfect synthesis between hilarity and despair but also leaves you feeling that we are all the victims of our own character.

In this play – as in most of the last four – the interest shifts slightly from the marital unhappiness of Celia and Toby to that of Miles, the Chairman of the school Governors, and Rowena, his jovially unfaithful wife ('They say at the Squash Club there are more bookings for her than there are for the squash courts'). This play starts with Miles visiting Celia and promising to save Toby's job as headmaster. One version of that scene propels Miles and Celia into a traumatic, agonised, adulterous affair. The other, better, version pushes Miles into a state of desperation that, even by Ayckbourn's own exacting standards, is unusually intense.

In fact, we see Miles and Rowena turning up five days later with the news that Toby's job has temporarily been saved. Unfortunately, there is no-one in the garden to greet them, a marital spat ensues and the prankish Rowena locks Miles in the garden shed. He is released by Sylvie, the warm-hearted housemaid upon whom almost everyone in these plays has designs, and when she urges him to get his revenge on Rowena by having an affaire himself he takes this as a hint and proposes that she joins him in a walk round the English coastline. She may, of course, fatally agree. But in this version she rejects his offer and he retreats back into the womb-like security of the shed where he is discovered five weeks later.

As a metaphor for a man in the throes of a mid-life crisis this is both painful and preposterous: a man going to pieces while surrounded by old lawnmowers and gardening-tools and with meals served through a little hatchway at the back. This is like Beckett with a touch of the ridiculous. The ultimate irony, of course, is that Rowena is convinced he has incarcerated himself to punish her and Celia believes it is out of unrequited passion for herself while only Sylvie knows the real truth. Finally, Rowena persuades him to emerge and begs him to come home and rejoin his family. He may, of course, say 'Yes'. But it is more interesting if he refuses and announces that he wants to go away and start all over again:

ROWENA: You can't start again. None of us can start again.

MILES: We can try. We have the choice. We must try. When you see that all the choices you've made so far are getting you nowhere, straight into a wall, you have to break out and start again.

ROWENA: Oh, God. Make all the same mistakes again?

MILES: Not necessarily.

ROWENA: Nothing changes. We are what we are. You can give up smoking or – wear different clothes or – get your nose altered but victims stay victims and bullies stay bullies – and people like me will go on being thoroughly selfish and frivolous and people like you, vulnerable people, you're never going to grow a thick skin. You might possibly learn to duck occasionally. That's the best you can hope for. But all in all *fait accompli*.

This is the clearest statement Ayckbourn makes in any of the plays: that it is impossible to escape from the cage of heredity, environment and circumstance that we call character. And he proves it in the conclusion when the characters all meet up at a Midnight Mass five years later. Sylvie is now married to Lionel. Toby and Celia are stuck in an irrevocable marital stalemate. Miles, having made his break for freedom, is living none too happily with a girl who won't give him a divorce while Rowena is still being laid from end to end by all of Bilbury. In one short scene, Ayckbourn conveys beautifully the ashen taste of a ruined marriage and ends with Miles confessing that Rowena is right: that it isn't possible to start one's life all over again.

Of course, no one play in the cycle contains the ultimate truth. But it is worth noting that even if Miles does go off for his coastal hike with Sylvie, it still ends in sad squabbles in a clifftop hut and an eventual return to the marital *status quo*. If there is any one message to be deduced from these multi-layered, seemingly contradictory, extraordinarily rich plays, it is that the pattern of our lives is determined by a multitude of things and that the illusion of chance is balanced by the imperatives of character. What is striking, however, is that the supposedly boulevard Ayckbourn is using the stage with the same kind of experimental freedom that writers like Robbe-Grillet and Sarraute brought to the *nouveau roman*. Ayckbourn may seem like an omniscient plotter mapping out the fate of his characters on the drawing-board but in the end this is less a thesis-drama than an extraordinarily open-ended exploration of human affairs, leaving us to decide whether chance or character has the upper-hand.

'A Chorus of Disapproval'

The writing of *Intimate Exchanges* was spread over a year. During that period, and in the immediate aftermath, Ayckbourn occupied himself with a host of other projects: a one-act play (*A Cut in the Rates*), a late-night revue (*Incidental Music*), a parodic thriller since withdrawn from circulation (*It Could Be Any One Of Us*), variations on an original work by Sheridan (*A Trip To Scarborough*) and a piece of music-theatre with Paul Todd (*The Seven Deadly Virtues*). But it was with *A Chorus of Disapproval*, presented in Scarborough in May, 1984 and at the Olivier Theatre in August, 1985, that Ayckbourn returned to his best form: a symmetrically shaped, psychologically acute and painfully funny play full of Ayckbourn's own brand of festive despair.

It uses an amateur operatic society production of Gay's *The Beggar's Opera* as its springboard. It also has another unacknowledged source: Gogol's 1836 Russian comedy, *The Government Inspector*. In that, a humble St Petersburg clerk arrives in a small provincial town, is mistaken for the Inspector General and is enthusiastically fêted to prevent him exposing the bribery and corruption that is rampant in local government. You can see the hero as a calculating impostor. In fact, he is a happy-go-lucky nonentity who becomes whatever people wish him to be: in that sense, he resembles the lowly, blundering mafioso in David Mamet's film, *Things Change*, who remarks 'They always like you when you're someone else.'

Guy Jones, the hero of *A Chorus of Disapproval*, is

very like Gogol's Khlestakov: a blank sheet upon whom the members of the community inscribe their own ruthlessness and ambition. When we first see him he has just enjoyed a modest triumph as Macheath in the Pendon Amateur Light Opera Society production of *The Beggar's Opera*. But the moment the curtain falls he is shunned by the rest of the cast and the play backtracks to explain why.

Guy has joined the Society as a lonely widower seeking to forge a new life after his wife's death. He is just a nice Guy who can't say No: a man whose moral conscience is no more than an echoing vacuum. The result is that he finds himself drawn into concurrent affaires with Hannah, the discontented wife of the production's shambling obsessive director, and with Fay Hubbard, a single-minded sexual swinger. Guy is also assumed to have insider knowledge of a proposed expansion by his firm which will greatly enhance the value of an adjacent piece of land which a number of people are hoping to buy cheap and sell dear. Partly because of his sexual availability and partly because he is thought to be acting on three different people's behalf over the land-sale, he finds himself rising within the company from the role of Crook-Fingered Jack to that of Filch and finally to the starring role itself. Guy's blank amorality promotes him within the company. The irony is that his personal rejection stems from his one act of altruism. He warns the land's owner of its rumoured purchase. This dishes Fay's husband, Ian, who has put both his wife and his role at Guy's disposal in the expectation of a return on his investment. In retaliation Ian tells the show's director, Dafydd, that he has been cuckolded by Guy. The hapless Guy winds up not only despised by lovers, friends and his director but also out of a job since his firm is contracting rather than expanding.

The social satire in the play works two ways. Obviously,

Ayckbourn is exposing the greed, graft, corruption and the casual sexual promiscuity of these outwardly respectable Pendon burghers. But the play also exposes Guy as the innocent nonentity who wreaks havoc by his simple inability to say 'No'. In one sense, he harks back to Colin in *Absent Friends*: the well-meaning, also bereaved hero who destroys a whole network of human relationships with a cheerfully vacuous smile. In another sense, he anticipates Jack McCracken in *A Small Family Business*: as Ayckbourn remarked to Ian Watson, 'I was chasing the theme of inner corruption inside a society and how an honest man in a dishonest society looks like the biggest rogue of all.' Ayckbourn is, in fact, both using Guy as a means of uncovering the rottenness of this microcosmic society and at the same time warning us that it is the naïve nonentities in life who are often the most dangerous of people. Guy's weakness itself becomes culpable. And the point is clinched in a crucial scene where Guy turns up in the garden of Rebecca Huntley-Pike, the wife of the owner of the disputed piece of land, to return a bribe of £500 that has mysteriously arrived in the post. When Mrs Huntley-Pike suggests that Guy might do nothing to dispel the rumours about the impending sale, he reacts with a touch of maidenly horror. On the other hand, Guy is encouraged to keep the bribe. 'Guy', says the stage-directions, 'stares at the envelope undecided. He half moves away. He stops. After a second or so he returns to the money. He takes it up and pockets it.' Thus does Ayckbourn neatly spear the wibbly-wobbly moral vacillations of the Guys of this world.

It is no accident that Guy steps out of this scene straight into the costume of the highwayman Macheath; and part of the charm of this play is the way Ayckbourn uses Gay's opera to underscore the bubbling corruption of English life. Gay's popular ballad-opera showed eighteenth-century low-life to be a mirror-image of Sir Robert Walpole's bent political administration. With equal wit, Ayckbourn shows respectable pillars of the community jovially pretending to be thieves and robbers and then behaving with the same shark-like rapacity as the characters they are impersonating.

Ayckbourn has revealed that his first idea was to use *The Vagabond King* as the framework, with 85 singers scattered incognito round the Scarborough auditorium and suddenly rising from their seats to sing a number. For purely practical reasons (objections from Equity and from the Rudolf Friml estate) he was forced to abandon that idea and substitute *The Beggar's Opera*. It is as well he did for what might have been a rather easy send-up of the whole world of amateur theatricals in the end becomes something much tougher, richer and more ironic with Gay's opera offering a stream of subliminal comment on the real action of the play. Macheath is torn between two women: in the same way, Guy is caught between Hannah and Fay (at one point seen wrangling over his underwear in a Pendon cafe) just as the original choice for Macheath divides his affections between a two-timing bouncy little stage-manager and a post-punk flirt. But none of the songs is arbitrarily chosen. Just after we have seen Dafydd, in his legal capacity, sounding out Guy about the land-deal we get a song from Peachum that ends:

> It ever was decreed, Sir,
> If Lawyer's Hand is fee'd, Sir,
> He steals your whole Estate.

And while Guy begins and ends the show singing, as a Macheath suddenly reprieved from hanging, 'The Wretch of To-day may be happy To-morrow', we come to see that Guy is actually left friendless, jobless and unreprieved. Ayckbourn, to his credit, doesn't hammer home the sundry parallels between his own work and Gay's: he simply offers a musical reinforcement of the idea that graft is embedded in English life.

Some people took the play to be a backstage farce on the lines of Michael Frayn's *Noises Off*: I see it as a Gogolian social comedy and proof of Ayckbourn's increasing interest in panoramic plays. He is now working with a wide-angled lens. But he also, in the characters of Hannah and Dafydd, pins down the pathos of a failed marriage with compassionate economy. Hannah (memorably incarnated at the National Theatre by Imelda Staunton as she crept apologetically into her own sitting-room) is a woman stunted by years of emotional neglect: Dafydd is an archetypal Welsh fanatic who has transferred his father's passion for Rugby football to the world of amateur theatre. You sense the aching loneliness of their marriage when Hannah reveals that the children have a Daddy-doll with whom they have tea, walks and supper ('I've stopped them taking it to bed with them now. I did think that was getting too much of a good thing'). But Ayckbourn also hints at a relationship haunted by some dark, unarticulated guilt. When Dafydd claims that Hannah is a woman of impenetrable frigidity who has virtually given up on sex ever since their wedding night, Guy cheerily points out that they still managed to have twins. To which Dafydd quickly replies 'Yes. Well we never talk about that. Never.' which leaves behind the unmistakable Strindbergian assumption that he may not be the actual father.

It is a sign of Ayckbourn's consummate maturity as a writer that he is able to weave so much sadness, pathos and bitterness into a play that is still a comedy. But then it is the very essence of late Ayckbourn that the dividing line between what is tragic and what is funny has become barely visible to the naked eye. One of the themes running through the play is that drama both feeds off life and excludes it: that the act of putting on a show, even *The Beggar's Opera* in Pendon, becomes all-consuming. Guy becomes methodically obsessive about his role as Crook-Fingered Jack even though it contains only one line. Dafydd graphically explains how getting the show on becomes paramount even when one's life and career are falling apart. And, in the best scene in the play, Ayckbourn demonstrates the devouring nature of theatre with heart-rending farce. While Dafydd uses Hannah and Guy to check the focus of his lighting, they are in the very middle of an agonising lovers' quarrel, in which Guy is trying to break off their relationship: thus the tromped, guileless, scruffy Dafydd, who has channelled whatever sexual urges he possessed into directing, potters about fixing lamps and perches, serenely oblivious to the fact that his wife and her lover are bitterly quarrelling as their relationship falls apart. You are caught between wind and water, laughter and tears as you so often are in Chekhov.

One argument used against Ayckbourn is that he despises his characters: that he presents us with what one critic called his 'familiar collection of frumps, nerds, creeps, would-be lovers and failed two-bit crooks from the suburbs.' But I sense neither loftiness nor derision in the writing. Steve Grant put it well in *Time Out* when he wrote that 'characters are observed in a gently objective way which reveals deficiency without moralising or rebuke.' Ayckbourn is certainly writing about crooked-ness, corruption, marital sadness and the mayhem caused by moral inertia. But he is writing a play, not reading us a lecture; and what he shows, with superb comic poignancy rather than sneery disdain, is how art consumes, shapes and organises life, leaving its participants infinitely sadder and wiser when it is over.

'Woman In Mind'

Women, it is commonly said, get a raw deal in our theatre. In many ways they do. But it is worth recalling that Ayckbourn's astonishing *Woman In Mind* opened at the Vaudeville in September, 1986 (having had its Scarborough premiere in May, 1985) during the same month as the following plays: Anne Devlin's *Ourselves Alone*, dealing with the dreams and disappointments of three Irish women abused and betrayed by Republican men; Nuria Espert's production of Lorca's *The House of Bernarda Alba* which graphically depicted immured, entrapped women in a male-dominated Andalusian society; and Michel Tremblay's Canadian play, *Albertine In Five Times* in which five actresses depicted the inner rage and torment that has disfigured one woman's life.

Ayckbourn's play does more than hold its own in such company: it offers one of the most sympathetic, imaginative, compassionate accounts of womanhood written by any British dramatist since the war (Terence Rattigan's *The Deep Blue Sea* is its most serious rival). But the key word is 'imaginative'. Ayckbourn has written constantly about masculine insensitivity towards women and in *Just Between Ourselves* even wrote a particularly abrasive comedy about a woman driven into a state of catatonia by an uncomprehending husband. But Ayckbourn rather shudders at the label of 'feminist dramatist' and what is notable is that he never preaches at us about the way women are mistreated or abused by men. He makes his points through imaginative sympathy and through offering us ineradicable stage-pictures that lodge in our consciousness. 'Art' Shelley once wrote, 'ought not to go about doing good by direct moral precept but should content itself with invigorating people's imaginations and trust the invigorated imagination to do the moral good afterwards.' That is precisely how Ayckbourn goes to work.

What makes *Woman In Mind* unique in my experience is that it sees the action entirely from the protagonist's point-of-view: in that sense, it is the theatrical equivalent of the first-person novel. The opening stage-directions make this abundantly clear: 'Darkness. We hear the sound of a woman moaning as she regains consciousness. As she opens her eyes, there is bright, afternoon garden sunlight. Throughout the play, we will hear what she hears; see what she sees. A subjective viewpoint therefore and one that may at times be somewhat less than accurate.'

The woman is Susan. She is recovering from concussion by a garden-rake and in the opening minute of the play converses with a doctor, Bill Windsor, in a blurred nonsense-language that has faint echoes of the real thing. 'December bee?' she imagines the doctor saying. It is that phrase which snaps her back into a kind of sense, which gives the play its sub-title and its last line and which surely calls to mind Ayckbourn's prototype, *Hamlet*, in which the Ghost cries 'Remember me.' Like *Hamlet*, *Woman in Mind* is a play in which the protagonist is driven into a state of madness and is prey to visitation by equivocal phantoms (all right, singular in Shakespeare, plural here) who may be uttering important truths or who may be evil enchanters. 'The spirit that I have seen,' says Hamlet, 'may be a devil and the Devil hath power to assume a pleasing shape.' That is precisely Susan's predicament: as she sits in her garden, she conjures up an alternative, fantasy-family who may indeed be diabolical figures in pleasing form. I would not wish to push the comparison too far: other obvious differences aside, *Hamlet* is not a play in which the whole action takes place inside the hero's head. But I cannot believe that Ayckbourn did not have Shakespeare in mind and that he was not attracted by the idea of showing madness as a condition partly induced by a Hamlet-like alienation from one's surroundings.

Many plays, of course, deal with the supernatural. The unique thing about *Woman In Mind* is that Susan's real family and her fantasy-family start out as polar opposites existing in different dimensions but gradually merge in her imagination as the play proceeds. Cunningly, Ayckbourn introduces us to her fantasy-family first: Andy her ideal-ised, athletic husband, Lucy her charming, easy-going daughter and Tony her good-looking brother who non-chalantly plays tennis at eleven in the morning with a glass of champers in his hand. Not only does this quickly establish the idea of her hallucinations and make her sympathetically recognisable (don't most people have similar Mittyesque dreams?). It also heightens the joke when we meet her appallingly real family. Her husband, Gerald, is a smug vicar who seeks to justify years of sexual and emotional neglect by the fact he is writing a 60-page history of the Parish. Muriel, her sister-in-law, is a grim, angular woman obsessed by the notion that her dead husband is trying to make contact with her and who is such a lousy cook she makes omelettes with Earl Grey tea. And Susan's son, Rick, is a member of a Trappist order in Hemel Hempstead who preserves his vow of silence on his increasingly rare visits home.

Ayckbourn is not above using an old *Blithe Spirit* joke in which remarks made to the unseen are misinterpreted by the corporeal. When Susan says to her fantasy-daughter, *à propos* a chair, 'Just put it there, darling, thank you' a surprised Bill Windsor takes the remark as addressed to him; and this has its pay-off later when he releases an apparently pent-up passion for Susan (or is this just her imagination?). But if the play were simply contrasting reality and fantasy, it would offer a one-way ticket to nowhere: what it actually says is that the inability to distinguish between the two is a clinical symptom of madness. As Susan becomes more desperate, her two worlds start to merge; and what is fascinating is how Ayckbourn suggests, through purely theatrical means, that the Barbara Cartland-style fantasy-family may be demons. Not only do they start to put words into Susan's mouth and anticipate her every thought: they start to behave in a demonstrably cruel manner. Early on in the play Ayckbourn plants the idea of a neighbouring dog whose howls are inaudible to Susan. Later Gerald comes in to announce that Mrs Ogle next door is distressed over the loss of her dog. A minute later, as the sky ominously darkens, Susan's fantasy-brother enters with a blood-stained game-bag the contents of which he significantly refuses to disclose. This is typical both of Ayckbourn's thrift and of the way he offers strong visual, as well as verbal, hints of the malign tenacity of Susan's phantom-family.

Obviously Ayckbourn is writing primarily in *Woman In Mind* about the symptoms and causes of madness. He has acknowledged the influence of Oliver Sacks's *The Man Who Mistook His Wife For A Hat*. He has also revealingly remarked that he chose a woman as his protagonist because people would treat a man very differently in that situation and presumably step in earlier to take remedial action. But although this is a more private, less panoramic play than *A Chorus of Disapproval* it is, I believe, still dealing with an important public issue: the failure of religion in the modern world to cope with mental distress.

Consider. Susan is the wife of a clergyman and clearly has a Manichean notion of good and evil. Almost her first reaction on discovering that she is unstable is to ask 'Why have I gone to hell? Why me, I've tried so terribly hard too. Terribly hard . . .' It is quite clear that Gerald has failed her on the most basic level as a husband. They sleep in separate beds, they don't kiss, they hardly even touch. And when Gerald asks if she is implying that sex is all that mattered in their relationship, she replies:

> All I'm saying is, that once that's gone – all *that* – it becomes important. Over-important really. I mean before when we – it was just something else we did together. Like gardening. Only now I have to do that on my own as well.

But if Gerald is a lousy husband he is an even worse cleric. Even when Susan has come to believe that she is demonically possessed, she makes it clear that Gerald is the last person that she would consult on spiritual matters. With his batty book on the history of the Parish since 1386, Gerald represents the kind of clergyman who regards himself as a custodian of tradition and history rather than a man of incandescent faith. It is interesting that Alan Bennett in his TV series, *Talking Heads*, wrote a powerful and not dissimilar monologue about a vicar's wife driven into the arms of an Asian grocer in Leeds while her husband largely concerned himself with the flower arrangements in church. What both Ayckbourn and Bennett seem to be saying is that too many churchmen are indifferent to the suffering that takes place under their own noses.

Susan's sister-in-law, Muriel, is also a believer. But in her case faith takes the form of an eccentric spiritualism and the unsustainable belief that her late husband, Harry, is trying to get through to her by inscribing messages on the ceiling. Even Gerald, in his waffly way, tries to point out that although Harry may be *there* in general he is not *here* in particular: immanent but not imminent. And Susan tartly points out that 'It does seem to me that God, in his infinite wisdom and with the entire cosmos to choose from is unlikely to base the Kingdom of Heaven around Muriel's bedroom.' For Muriel, religion is simply a form of psychic self-delusion. As for Rick, who has retreated into a Trappist order in Hemel Hempstead from which he suddenly emerges to announce that he is married and about to make a new life in Thailand, he simply represents the declension of religion into a narcissistic sectarianism. I doubt that Ayckbourn sat down to write a tractarian work about the failure of religion to measure up to mental crisis. But what the play actually shows is Susan deserted, in her hour of crisis, by God's representative and Christian love. The consequence is that she falls into the arms of the Devil: quite literally, since she ends up being made love to by Satanic Andy (her onetime dream-husband) on her own back lawn in the middle of a thunderstorm at three in the morning. And any doubt that Andy and his accomplices are diabolical is dispelled when a fire breaks out in Gerald's study destroying all but one page of his precious book and a sign appears on his sister's bedroom ceiling with the immemorial injunction, apparently from her late husband, 'Knickers off Muriel.'

With this play the dated notion of Ayckbourn as a mild-mannered farceur is decisively laid to rest. He is writing about madness, menopausal female frustration and the failure of religion to do its proper work in the world. The miracle is that the play still manages to be hugely funny: the very factors that oppress Susan are made biliously comic and there are numerous little Ayckbourn curlicues, such as Bill Windsor's touching blindness to the fact that his wife is quite obviously having an affaire with his senior partner.

The production of this play also demolished another myth: that Ayckbourn's plays are invariably better in Scarborough and are somehow diluted by starry West End presentation. Ursula Jones gave a fine performance as poor demented Susan in Scarborough: Julia McKenzie gave a matchless one in London filled with shrewdness, longing, hope, sexiness and a terrible despair. But it was also much easier to establish the otherness of Susan's dream-world behind a proscenium-arch than it was at the Stephen Joseph Theatre in the Round. At the Vaudeville, Roger Glossop created a strange, sinister, gauzy, Barrie-sque ambience full of receding poplars, marble statuary and Byzantine mazes. It was an apt image for the state of Susan's tortured, intricate mind and a perfect metaphor for a brave, disturbing, challenging play that suggested one of our greatest crimes is a kind of moral myopia that allows us to be oblivious to the sufferings in our midst.

'A Small Family Business'

Ayckbourn is not the first dramatist to see a solid English family as a symbol of conscienceless corruption. J. B. Priestley's *An Inspector Calls* (1946) takes apart the smug, safe, mahogany-and-leather world of the Birlings and shows how every member of the family shares responsibility for the suicide of a young girl: Father has sacked her from his factory, Daughter has had her discharged from a shop, Son has seduced her, Mother has had her barred from charity. Everyone shares in the moral guilt.

A Small Family Business – written specifically for the Olivier Theatre where it had its premiere in 1987 and Ayckbourn's first play not written for Scarborough in almost a quarter of a century – has certain affinities with Priestley's play: an inspector even calls though he is not remotely like Priestley's steely embodiment of conscience. But what makes Ayckbourn's play uniquely his is its brilliant combination of morality and farce. It is as political as Caryl Churchill's *Serious Money* in its devastating assault on the way we live now and on the way the entrepreneurial values we have been told to foster have become a mask for fraud, theft and wholesale self-deceit: by the end of a richly-plotted evening the words 'family' and 'business' have acquired sinister *mafioso* overtones. But the play, although it deals with bribery, blackmail, theft, industrial espionage, sado-masochism, drug-trafficking and homicide, is still biliously funny. In its use of a split-level suburban set to suggest the different houses of various members of the same family, it also affords wonderful scope for fluidity of action. It reminds one yet again that Ayckbourn the playwright is as much a master-craftsman as a shipwright or a wheelwright.

It may be a morality play but it is anything but simple-minded: indeed it is compact with irony. On the surface, it shows honest, upright, undevious Jack McCracken taking over the family furniture firm, Ayres and Graces, and delivering a brisk moral homily on the importance of Faith and Trust. But Jack is forced to compromise his own principles when a slimy private detective, Hough, arrives to announce that Samantha, Jack's teenage daughter, has been caught shoplifting. After a good deal of huffing and puffing, Jack is eventually forced to buy off

Hough with the promise of a security job at Ayres and Graces. To his horror, Jack also discovers that the family produce is being pirated and appearing on foreign markets under different labels. It transpires that it is a cunning family racket operated by Jack's brother-in-law, Desmond, who sells off the unlabelled furniture via the back door, and by Jack's brother, Cliff, and his wife Anita, who then buy the furniture 'legitimately' and resell it to an Italian firm called Rivetti. Since Hough has also discovered the racket, Jack is forced to act as bagman for the family, offering the private eye ever larger sums to procure his silence. When Hough asks for an unrealistically large amount, Jack emphatically draws the line at murder: somewhat needlessly since Hough has been inadvertently killed by Jack's wife and two daughters. The play ends, as it has begun, with a celebratory family party at which Jack accedes – after an initial show of reluctance – to the use of the furniture distribution network as an outlet for the Rivetti drug-ring.

Obviously Ayckbourn is writing about the slippery nature of moral compromise: the way a concession on a relatively small matter leads to a series of ever-greater concessions until an upright businessman ends up as a mafioso *capo*. He is also showing the Ten Commandments going down like ninepins.

Honour thy father and thy mother; but not the least of Desmond's sins is that he is swindling the firm he has inherited from his own father for the fairly ludicrous purpose of opening his own restaurant in the Balearics, notwithstanding the fact he is almost as bad a cook as Muriel in *Woman In Mind*.

Thou shalt not kill; but the family agrees that the inquisitive Hough must be dispatched by a hit-man, Jack's wife and daughters do the actual deed and Jack himself finally pays the market-price for the disposal of the unwanted corpse by the Rivetti Brothers.

Thou shalt not commit adultery; but Anita, who is into whips and black leather, keeps herself and Cliff in luxury through the selling of sexual favours though, when accused of prostitution, fudges the issue by saying 'You can accept heartfelt tokens of appreciation, that's all. But they've got to be heartfelt.'

Thou shalt not steal; but everyone in the family does, from Desmond who is actually organising the theft of his own firm's furniture, to Jack's wife, Poppy, who brings home paper clips and pencils from her office.

Thou shalt not covet thy neighbour's house nor his ox nor his ass nor anything that is thy neighbour's; but Cliff and Desmond's whole lives are built around covetousness and even Poppy is not above accepting some of the benefits of Anita's immoral earnings.

In *Way Upstream* Ayckbourn wrote a fable about evil. In *Woman In Mind* he showed the fallibility of religion. In this play he demonstrates what happens to a world devoid of God or even any basic moral precepts. But Ayckbourn is also a master ironist and depicts Jack McCracken not simply as a good man drawn insidiously into a network of corruption but as a man who in some ways is the architect of his own downfall. He makes a fine speech at the beginning about the importance of Effort and Trust. At the same time, Ayckbourn implies that his brand of inflexible morality makes no allowance for human weakness and that he is a negligent father whose indifference to Samantha (to whom he hardly speaks) has pushed her into the reclusive world of drugs. Jack's initial refusal to trade with Hough and allow his daughter to be prosecuted ('Where does it end, for one thing?' he prophetically enquires) may be morally correct. It is also unfeeling as his remark 'Look, to hell with Sammy, there's a principle at stake' graphically indicates. With considerable subtlety, Ayckbourn portrays Jack as a man whose honesty is theoretically admirable but whose indifference to his daughter is culpable; and this is clearly expressed through the drug issue which runs through the whole play. It is one of the play's numerous bitter ironies that it is Samantha who gives Hough the push into the tin-bath that kills him and that, as the stage-directions tell us, 'one gathers she was in a fairly dazed state when she started'. And, in a resonant final image, while Jack is agreeing to deals with the drug-trafficking Rivettis and the family is celebrating its solidarity, Samantha is alone upstairs in the bathroom mainlining.

That is the kind of effect it is very hard to convey in cold print. But one of the triumphs of the play is the way Ayckbourn uses the multiple rooms of his split-level set to suggest that people in one area are unaware of what is going in another. He uses this to hilarious effect at the beginning with the whole family crowded into Jack's sitting room for a party while Jack is stampeding through the hall and up the stairs divesting himself of his clothes and telling his wife that he is Erik the Hairy Viking with his big 'meatey axey'. Finally, Poppy retreats into the sitting-room where the trouserless Jack rampageously follows her only to discover a roomful of guests. This doesn't merely get the play off to a rousing start. It immediately establishes Jack as a sympathetic, red-blooded guy with whose physical predicament we can all identify; which is vital if we are to follow him in his labyrinthine moral predicament as the play progresses.

But Ayckbourn's most potent theatrical device is seen later on when Jack is busy rushing from one house to another trying to raise more loot to blackmail Hough while Hough himself is prowling through Jack's house trying to find a briefcase stuffed with notes. At one moment, we see Jack on ground level alone in Cliff's house while the creepy, reptilian, insidious Hough is tiptoeing into Jack's upper-storey bedroom where Poppy is hiding. A part of us wants to cry out a warning to Jack to go to his wife's rescue; except of course that Jack is in another house altogether. Ayckbourn plays with the properties of space much as Shakespeare does with the duality of time: both space and time have a double existence on the theatrical and the real level. Ayckbourn also plays skilfully on the audience's complex emotional and moral reactions to Hough's death. In practice I have noticed it is greeted with a mixture of horrified shock and yelping amusement; and the truth is that one side of us wants to see this perverted, rapacious monster, wrestling with the three women for possession of the briefcase, get his just deserts while another side of us withdraws in revulsion. To play on two emotions simultaneously is one of the highest dramatic skills. Ayckbourn does it here beautifully, not only by building up the suspense from moment to moment (we know something dreadful is going to happen but we half hope it won't) but also by having Jack inveighing against murder ('That's it. That's it. We have reached the pit. We have touched the sewage. We are back on all fours.') only seconds before it is about to be committed in his own house.

When Poppy finally confronts Jack with a corpse in the bloodstained bath all she can feebly say is 'I'm very sorry, Jack' (a line that gets a big laugh). But one of the points Ayckbourn is making in the play is that our moral sensibilities have become blunted because we constantly clothe things in euphemistic language. Jack says to his wife concerning the corpse 'We're going to get things cleared up and then we're going to put all this lot behind us' as if a dead body were simply a bit of unsavoury garbage. Earlier, Jack, clutching a suitcase containing five thousand pounds in notes, refers to it as 'Just paper. Bits of – bits of paper.' Anita, who is an S and M pro if ever there was one, conveniently describes herself as 'an amateur'. And people constantly talk of 'salting it away' when they are referring to money they have stolen. Until we use the right language, Ayckbourn suggests, we shall never be able to confront the consequences of our actions; and until we stop hero-worshipping the criminal (Jack's elder daughter, Tina finds her respect for her wimpy husband has shot up ever since she discovered he was involved in the family racket) we shall sink further into a state of moral vacuity.

But again Ayckbourn's great gift is that he shows rather than tells. He doesn't harangue his audience about the evils of capitalism. He simply offers us a comic fable about a recognisably ordinary family whose materialistic hunger has allowed them to slither into crime. He also uses humour as the bait with which to hook his audience. I recall sitting at the Olivier behind a middle-aged couple who as the play started nudged each other with delight in the expectation of a harmless diversion. As the evening went on, they still laughed but without quite the same conspiratorial mutual glee as they showed at the beginning as if the argument of the play were penetrating their comfortable exteriors. I would guess that was precisely the effect Ayckbourn was after.

'Henceforward'

Ayckbourn is not a reassuring writer. His special talent

is for stating uncompromising truths in a theatrically acceptable manner; and indeed all his recent work treads a delicate tightrope between comedy and despair (rightly so since as the heroine says in Peter Shaffer's *Lettice and Lovage*, 'Without danger there is no theatre'). But in *Henceforward* (which had its Scarborough premiere in July, 1987 and opened at London's Vaudeville Theatre in November, 1988) Ayckbourn has written his bleakest play yet: one that still manages to wring laughter out of desperation but also one that presents us, both in terms of its governing images and its prevailing ideas, with a pessimistic vision.

Three central, and closely related, themes thread their way through the play. One concerns the dilemma of the creative artist – in this case, a composer called Jerome – parastically feeding off the lives, the emotions and needs of those closest to him. It is a problem that has guiltily obsessed writers down the ages and that Ibsen dealt with hauntingly in his last play, *When We Dead Awaken*. There, an aged sculptor, Rubek, is confronted by a former model, Irene, whose palpable human love he has sacrificed to the demands of his calling. 'Before all else,' he says, 'I was an artist. And I was sick – sick with a longing to create the one great work of my life. It was to be called "The Day of Resurrection".' In just such a manner Ayckbourn's Jerome, whose governing desire is 'to express the feeling of love in an abstract musical form', finally rejects proffered human love in order to capture what he sees as its essence on his digital keyboard.

Allied to the artist's specific dilemma is the universal theme of modern man's increasing subordination to technology (and the play is set in the not-too-distant future): as Charles Osborne wrote, 'we are all programmed, Ayckbourn seems to be telling us, no longer using but used by the technology we have created.' Thus Jerome lives in a computerised bunker surrounded by keyboards, synclaviers and video-screens flashing up messages of desperation from a beleaguered friend. Jerome is even serviced by an android, NAN 300F (which in the first act resembles his wife and in the second that of an idealised fiancée-companion) to which he relates more easily than people.

Closely allied to that is the notion of a society that is on the edge of breakdown: a Dystopian vision of hell in which outer London suburbs like Edgware are policed by mobs of vigilante feminists (the Daughters of Darkness) with purple stripes tattooed across their faces and in which even Kilburn is filled with regular armed patrols and masses of security cameras. Ayckbourn recounted to Ian Watson the story of an art historian in West Yorkshire who was frightened to walk to the shops because of the primitive tribes roaming around his house. Ayckbourn is projecting into the future the fear many people have today of walking the streets. But he is also suggesting that, even inside this *Clockwork Orange* society, lonely, isolated individuals still struggle to create art.

Ayckbourn's vision is dark, strong and clear. The problem he encounters is that, theatrically, it takes a good deal of time to establish both the precise nature of this nightmare universe and the racking, stunted solitude of Jerome himself: the result is that the first act plays a little slowly and that it is only in the second a genuine tension arises from the conflict between man and machine. In the second act – with the introduction of fresh characters – there is also a much stronger element of social comedy to alleviate the prevailing harshness. Oddly enough, the play gets funnier as it gets blacker and as it starts to exploit Henri Bergson's proposition that 'We laugh every time a person gives us the impression of being a thing': in this play, we laugh the more things start to behave like people.

In fact, the play starts with Jerome tinkering with NAN 300F – the prototype for an automatic child-minder that never went into full production – and Ayckbourn gets some good laughs both out of the sight of Jerome with his hand up her skirt and out of the android's split personality: she has both the brisk solicitude of a nanny and the reproving tones of a deceived wife. Jerome, it transpires, has been left by his wife Corinna and their daughter Geain (pronounced Jane) and in the four years since their departure has suffered a monumental creative block. He has even been forbidden to see his own daughter. And in an effort to convince the Department of Child Wellbeing and Corinna (both due to pay him a visit) that he is a fit father, he is auditoning a young actress, Zoe, to play the role of the perfect fiancée-companion and to help create an impression of domestic bliss. Zoe is touched by his story, goes to bed with him but is appalled the next morning to discover that every moment of their lovemaking has been recorded by Jerome. Since he cannot even understand her moral qualms about having their most intimate experiences recorded, reprocessed and used as raw artistic material, she sweeps out into vigilante-patrolled Edgware. Jerome decides the only solution is to reprogramme NAN in Zoe's image also using her vocal rhythms and inflexions.

Ayckbourn skilfully interweaves his three dominant themes in this act. Jerome is trying mechanically to achieve the sound of love but, in human terms, is incapable of understanding it. His life has also been taken over by blinking, flashing screens and machines that put a barrier between himself and reality; his musical friend, Lupus, keeps appearing on the video-screen with cries for help which Jerome easily ignores. And the menace of the streets is indicated by Zoe's arrival torn and bleeding after an encounter with the Daughters of Darkness who proceed to throw bricks at the barricaded shutters. But although the ideas lock securely into place it is, unusually for Ayckbourn, an act rather lacking in narrative momentum. We are exactly halfway through before we discover precisely why Jerome has hired Zoe and there is a faint air of doodling about the proceedings. Ayckbourn is so busy giving us the atmosphere – as in Jerome's remark that 'Since they fully automated the hypermarket, I don't think I've spoken to anyone for months' – that he almost forgets the obligation to keep the story driving onwards.

The second act is much richer both because it reminds us that Jerome's obsession with technology is universal and because it sharpens the conflict of man versus machine. It also *embodies* the central issue of the play in a chilling, funny horrendous image: the spectacle of NAN reprogrammed as Zoe dressed like an old-style Southern belle and reacting to every remark made to her by Corinna and Mervyn, the berk from Social Services, with a chirpy, robotical brightness. It is funny for sound, Bergsonian reasons: the way, for instance, NAN-Zoe greets everyone mechanically with a cry of 'Hallo. Hallo. Hallo. Welcome. Welcome. Welcome' like a demented parody of a TV chat-show host. It is chilling (in the way the first act isn't) because we already have seen the gauche, dippy, sexy, flesh-and-blood Zoe before she was turned into this Superdoll. And it is horrendous exactly because we see that Jerome is more at ease with the programmed android than he was with the unpredictable, unprogrammed Zoe. In the first act, Ayckbourn sometimes seems to be illustrating a thesis: in this act, he shows the consequences of his ideas in action.

But Ayckbourn also brings on new characters in this act and widens the social range. What is tragic in Jerome becomes comic in Mervyn, whose pocket-phones are always bleeping at inappropriate moments and whose Italian thermal singlet has to be unravelled at one point as if it were the intestines of a dead sheep. Jerome's daughter, Geain, also turns out not to be some idealised Goldilocks but a booted, belted, studded, vaguely threatening thug whom her father unkindly compares to a 'transvestite truck-driver' (another sign of his inability to cope with reality though in this case one can hardly blame him). And Corinna turns out to be not quite the rancorous, vindictive monster we had been led to expect but a surprisingly vulnerable, 40-year-old bank manager who sits crying in her office and who actually wants Jerome back.

These are not merely standard comic reversals. Ayckbourn is making the point that humankind is complex, contradictory, confused, messy and, above all, phenomenally *interesting* in a way that machines never can be. Jerome's whole tragedy is that he cannot see that; and it is symbolised by the moment where he defends the NAN 300F model even though production was aborted after one of them put a baby in a microwave oven:

MERVYN: I don't see how you can possibly take the side of a machine against a human being.

JEROME: Against most human beings, very easily. If human beings behaved a bit less like human beings and a bit more like machines, we'd all be better off . . . .

That is Jerome's predicament in a nutshell; but the full tragedy of his position only becomes clear in the closing seconds. Corinna's reiterated cry of 'Love' in conversation has given him the vocal pattern he needs for his perfect sound; and at the end he rejects wife, daughter and life itself to play with the synthesised sound, oblivious to the fact that missiles are clanging against the shutters and the Daughters of Darkness have penetrated his inner sanctum. As the stage directions indicate: 'He sits all alone. And realizes how alone he is.'

I doubt that the play will ever become a loved and endlessly revived part of the Ayckbourn canon: it is both too technically complex and spiritually pessimistic. But it is still, after its hesitant first act, a remarkable play in that it dramatises Ayckbourn's own fears and guilts and in that it projects us not into sci-fi fantasy but into a just recognisable future. It makes us ask whether we are, literally, enthralled by our word-processors and domestic computers, whether we do actually prefer rational machines to irrational human beings and whether the streets of our towns and cities are becoming as bogey-haunted as the woods in a Grimm fairy-tale. Ayckbourn has written many more amenable plays. But *Henceforward* is a theatrical early-warning system of considerable prophetic power.

'Man of the Moment'

Ayckbourn never stands still. With each new play what he does, like any artist, is to elaborate on his obsessive themes and, at the same time, explore new ideas and experiment technically. He knows that each play has to appeal directly to his faithful Scarborough audience. At the same time, he is always trying to push the frontiers of drama outwards.

Alan Ayckbourn

Man of the Moment (his 35th major, full-length play
which had its Scarborough premiere in August, 1988) is a
perfect demonstration of this and a brilliantly achieved
piece of work. It continues the exploration of the nature
of evil which really began with *Way Upstream* in 1981. It
also shows Ayckbourn, as in *A Small Family Business*,
wrestling with the problem of writing a comedy that
includes a violent death. But he is doing much else in this
play. He is dealing with a crucial reversal of moral values
in our society that elevates villains to heroic status and
that quickly throws true heroes on to the discard pile (with
extraordinary topicality the play opened in Scarborough
at the time of a row about whether members of the Royal
Family should attend the gala opening of the film, *Buster*,
about a former Great Train Robber). He is also tackling
head-on the way television distorts and manipulates reality
and often ignores the real truth about human beings. And,
most daringly of all, he is writing a play in which much of
the action is retrospective: not since Ibsen's *Rosmersholm*
can I recall a play that depended so much for its effect on
a recapitulation of past events and the way they continue
to haunt the present.

The framework for the play is an attempt by a pushy,
ambitious young TV presenter, Jill Rillington, to bring
together an erstwhile bank robber, Vic Parks, and a one-
time bank clerk, Douglas Beechey, who 'had a go' at him
during a raid seventeen years previously. Vic, having
served a nine-year sentence, is now a media star with two
television series, a best-selling, sanitised autobiography
and a huge popular following to his credit. He also lives
part of the year, with his wife and family, in a Spanish
Mediterranean villa where the TV programme, *Their
Paths Crossed*, is to be shot. Douglas, who enjoyed a
brief, transitory fame as a popular hero seventeen years

200

ago, is now a forgotten figure working for a firm of double-glazing consultants in his native Purley. It turns out that his act of heroism in tackling the bank-robbing Vic was prompted by his unrequited passion for a beautiful bank clerk, Nerys. In the ensuing mêlée, Nerys was shot in the face by Vic and scarred for life. Because Douglas was the one person who continued visiting her in hospital, they ended up getting married and are now contented with their lot, although they have forsworn sex for the last fifteen years and Nerys lives as a virtual recluse.

Jill Rillington's purpose in bringing Doug and Vic together again is to contrast the dowdy Purley existence of one with the glitzy celebrity lifestyle of the other and to depict Doug as a man envious of his former antagonist's success. But she is baffled at every turn by Doug's apparent dullness and admiration for Vic. History, however, repeats itself when Vic, an unreformed egotistical monster, is confronted by a wild onslaught from Doug. Vic, who throughout bullies and dominates the women around him, stands jeeringly by while the kid's nurse, Sharon, attempts to drown herself out of love for him. He wrestles with his wife, Trudy, who is outraged by his callousness. Vic is butted in the midriff by Doug, topples into the pool and is dragged under water by Sharon and subsequently dies. But, at the end, we see the poolside events reconstructed by actors for the benefit of the TV cameras and a studio audience. What, in effect, was murder is presented as a needless accident with Jill, who has missed the real story, solemnly telling the viewers 'That night marked not only the end of a life but the end of a living legend.'

As so often, Ayckbourn is dealing with good and evil and indicating that we live in a society that ignores the former and rewards the latter. Unlike Vince in *Way Upstream* who too nakedly embodies the Fascist spirit in action, Vic in this play is an instantly recognisable figure: the one-time criminal whose gift of the gab has turned him into a popular media star. But Ayckbourn's key point is that we sentimentalise such figures by turning them into adored celebrities. He makes it quite clear that Vic owes his public fame to the way he articulates a kind of late-Eighties populist aggression: Jill recalls at the end Vic's advice to a young viewer, 'Don't complain to me that people kick you when you're down. It's your own fault for lying there, isn't it.' That, in slightly exaggerated form, catches all too accurately the *sauve-qui-peut* philosophy of Britain today. Vic is presented as the people's champion; but we also see him, in private, as a bullying vulgarian who treats his wife, the children's nanny and the Spanish maid with a similar patronising contempt. In a line of stunning perceptiveness – one of the best in all Ayckbourn – Trudy remarks: 'He's like a lot of men I've met. They don't quite know what to do with a woman when they've got her so they shout at her.' And in a wickedly funny foretaste of the final drowning (and in an apt comment on TV values) Ayckbourn at the end of the first act shows Vic and the rest ignoring the fact that the Spanish gardener, Ruy, is struggling for his life in the pool and thereby interrupting a crucial establishing shot. The scene is played as farce and had the audience at Scarborough collapsing with laughter; but it nonetheless subliminally contributes to the atmosphere of evil and is part of the pattern of ironic repetition Ayckbourn uses throughout the play.

David Hare pointed out recently that 'What's noticeable so far about the most popular plays of this decade is that they borrow their vitality from immoral characters'. It is certainly true that evil is theatrically seductive whilst goodness is damnably hard to write about; but Ayckbourn, through the character of Douglas Beechey, shows it can be done. He doesn't disguise the fact that Douglas is, in some ways, sad, comic and absurd: a pullovered Purley figure rather too contented with his dank semi-detached and all too ready to be the dupe of the TV smart-asses who, back home, had him running round the park as if they wanted to finish him off. But Ayckbourn also shows us that there is an instinctive chivalry about the man that is wholly admirable and that behind the suburban dullness there is a remarkable story if only anyone has the patience and empathy to dig it out: needless to say it is not the professional interviewer, who regards him simply as camera-fodder, that does it but the cowed and sympathetic Trudy. As played by Jon Strickland at Scarborough, Douglas seemed the very embodiment of nervous knight-errantry; and it says something about Ayckbourn's capacity to tap a popular sentiment that people used to accost the actor in the street and congratulate him on standing up for quiet decency and goodness.

Ayckbourn also writes, with the disinterestedness of a relative outsider, about the tendency of television to bend, manipulate and distort reality. It is amazing how few plays television has spawned considering its enormous impact on all our lives: Martin Allen's *Particular Friendships* and Brian Thompson's *Turning Over* are the only examples from recent years that spring to mind. Ayckbourn makes some fairly obvious, but still valid, jokes about the way events are staged and set up specially for the cameras: the poolside reunion, for instance, of Vic and Doug which blithely ignores the fact that they have been recapping past events for most of a morning off-camera. But Ayckbourn makes the much bigger point that television is a kind of game and that it is important to know the rules. Ayckbourn is not given to set speeches but Vic has a long passage about how to bend a television interview to one's own advantage, such as not pausing so that there is no room for editing, that, as Robin Thornber pointed out, 'must become a classic text for media studies courses.'

The play's fundamental irony, however, is that Jill Rillington, the TV interviewer, knows in advance what she wants her programme to say, is disappointed and frustrated when reality turns out to be otherwise and then misses the real story when some of her initial suspicions are confirmed. She hauls Douglas out to Spain in the hope of catching his resentment towards and envy of the gold-plated shit, Vic. She then finds that Douglas is dismayingly happy as he is and has not the slightest desire to have a particle of the good life enjoyed by Vic: she even finds he has no desire to travel abroad, least of all to Sweden:

> DOUGLAS: Not attracted sorry. Despite their standard of living they always look a rather glum sort of people, don't you think? They certainly do on the television.
> JILL: Well, you can't always go by everything (she checks herself). Possibly.

But Ayckbourn delivers his final blow to the cathode-ray tube when he contrasts the messy, ugly, farcical circumstances of Vic's drowning with the clean, tidied-up, orderly version restaged by actors for the benefit of the TV audience. The fat and rather ungainly nanny is now delectably slim (though she has also become 'this simple, semi-literate version from Macclesfield'), the house-servants are more authentically Spanish and even the country and western music issuing from the house is now more romantic than it originally was. Everything is false, untrue, mythical; and we, by being treated as if we were the studio-audience, become conspirators in this fraudulent attempt to recreate reality.

This is Ayckbourn at the top of his bent: using comedy both to state fundamental truths about human nature and also to send us out of the theatre questioning the kind of topsy-turvy values of our society and the mendacity of our most popular form of communication. It is also a phenomenally daring play in that two-thirds of it consists of recapitulated action that explains precisely why people behave as they do in the present. But, with each new play, Ayckbourn seems to become a richer writer. He uses drama to say disquieting things while still taking his audience with him. He is a comic pessimist, a farcical Diogenes who takes an increasingly sombre view of the state of modern Britain while still giving audiences the tonic of laughter and a good night out.

'The Revengers' Comedies'

'It's my fiftieth birthday this year, so I thought something rather ambitious was in order.' Thus Ayckbourn, with an uncharacteristic flourish, announced *The Revengers' Comedies*: a two-part, five-hour play that had its premiere in Scarborough in June 1989, three months after Ayckbourn had reached his own half-century. In one sense, it sounds like a return to the inordinate scale of *The Norman Conquests* or *Sisterly Feelings*. The difference is that, on this occasion, the two parts have to be seen together and in the correct chronological sequence in order to make sense.

Revenge is clearly the theme: something that has fascinated Ayckbourn ever since he directed both *A View From The Bridge* and *'Tis Pity She's a Whore* at the National

Theatre. And, lest we were in any doubt, the Scarborough programme was peppered with quotations that emphasised both the futility of revenge and, intriguingly, the fact that it is a particularly feminine weapon. Bacon's humanist condemnation ('A man that studieth revenge keeps his own wounds green, which otherwise would heal and do well') was balanced by quotations from Nietzsche ('In revenge and in love woman is more barbarous than man'), Molière ('A woman always has her revenge ready') and many others, implying a sexual distinction in the operation of revenge. Not the least fascinating feature of the play is seeing Ayckbourn, the instinctive feminist, for the first time creating a female character of ruthless, implacable evil.

Ayckbourn is a matchless deviser of plots but, on this occasion, there is a clear and obvious source: the Patricia Highsmith novel, and subsequently Hitchcock film, *Strangers on a Train*, in which a totally innocent party gets caught up in a madman's obsessive desire for a double revenge-murder. But Ayckbourn begins, characteristically, on a note of brilliant comedy. Henry Bell, a sad little man who has been deserted by his wife and ousted from his job in a multi-national by the aggressively opportunist Bruce Tick, is about to throw himself off Albert Bridge. Just as he is about to kill himself he hears a cry for help from another would-be suicide, Karen Knightly. Self-slaughter turns to an act of Samaritanism as he rescues the impaled woman and together they repair to a motorway café to compare notes. Henry has been stung by the loss of his job. Karen is grieving over the loss of her lover, a married West Country farmer, who has apparently been lured away by his scheming and devious wife, Imogen Staxton-Billing. It is Karen who suggests that, instead of lamenting their fate, they each take care of each other's problem. Karen will, in some unspecified way, 'do for' the appalling Tick if Henry will wreak appropriate revenge on the Machiavellian Imogen. Shell-shocked by the Albert Bridge encounter, and lured into bed by the wily Karen at her 58-room family mansion, Henry dazedly agrees.

It is a blithe premise for a comedy in that it thrusts the twin protagonists into totally alien and unfamiliar worlds; and much of the fun lies in seeing how they either do or don't adjust. The criss-cross plotting is beautifully done with wealthy, beautiful Karen turning herself into a flat-heeled frump in order to get taken on as Bruce Tick's temporary secretary. Ayckbourn makes us relish her deviousness by depicting the dreaded Tick as an arrogant, opinionated, eructating boor and by showing Karen herself to be a woman of matchless ingenuity: as in *Les Liaisons Dangereuses* we are drawn into the conspiracy by a delight in tactics. Karen's method is to ruin Tick's home-life by sending breathy messages down the phone to his wife and sending sexy nighties through the post, suggesting that an affaire is in full swing. But Ayckbourn's most audacious stroke, as in *A Small Family Business* and *Man of the Moment*, is to make us virtual accomplices to murder. We long to see Tick get what's coming to him; and, in the superb scene where Karen (exuding a leggy glamour) interrupts a rendezvous between Tick and his estranged wife, we experience an horrific exhilaration as Tick slumps dead to the floor with a heart attack. This is top-flight Ayckbourn in that it manages to induce in the audience a macabre pleasure and a moral shock *both at the same time*.

But Ayckbourn gets double value out of his plot by contrasting Karen's smooth success in the world of office politics with Henry's visible discomfort with a life of rural grandeur. Kitted out in new togs by Karen, he is mistaken by the locals for her accountant. Left to his own devices in the vast, gloomy family mansion (also occupied by Karen's strangely laid-back brother) he finds himself at the mercy of a dragon-housekeeper and a nervously incompetent apprentice servant: Ayckbourn's gift for visual humour (reaching way back to *Mr Whatnot*) comes out superbly in the scene where the terrified, butter-fingered servant-girl finds even the dispatch of cornflakes to the plate too much for her. But Henry's greatest crisis comes when he discovers that his intended victim, Imogen Staxton-Billing, is not the diabolical siren he had been led to expect but a deceived and neglected wife with whom he falls instantly in love. Again one is reminded of *Les Liaisons Dangereuses* where we see the hero driven by a wily female tactician into exacting revenge on a provincial wife, only to become ensnared by love.

This first play strikes me as a small masterpiece built around a series of deftly-woven contrasts: city versus country; female guile versus masculine helplessness; cold-hearted ruthlessness versus awakening tenderness. On the one hand, Ayckbourn gleefully enlists us in Karen's cause by making her victim a prize Tick (the kind of man who advertises his marital fidelity by announcing of his wife, 'I leave my balls back there with her in Sunningdale'). On the other hand, he makes us care about the growingly tender relationship between Henry and Imogen, who are thrown together after she has been severed from her horse in a riding accident. We want one part of the revenge-pact to succeed just as much as we want the other half to fail. But Ayckbourn also gets maximum value out of the contrast between the corporate warren of multi-national life and the enforced intimacy of the countryside where, as Karen says, 'You can't stop seeing people just because you've slept with them – otherwise you'd end up a hermit.'

The State of the Nation

The first half of *The Revengers' Comedies* is superb: the second half is less satisfying. Karen has accomplished her mission: Henry has no wish to fulfil his side of the bargain. So where does the plot have to go? In fact, Ayckbourn shows Karen worming her way to the top of the corporate heap by all kinds of devious tricks reminiscent of *How To Succeed In Business Without Really Trying*. It's all quite fun but you feel there is no reason for Karen to stay on in London once she has done what she set out to do. The rural scenes work far better since poor, blundering Henry gets the wrong end of the stick and spreads a rumour that Imogen's husband is having an improbable affaire with the Knightly's slightly dim-witted servant-girl. Henry has sullied the man's honour and broken the ethical code of country life and, in a scene of wonderfully dotty inventiveness, he is challenged to a duel which takes place under cover of a woodland shooting-party. The scene (arguably the first duel in modern drama since *Three Sisters*) is lunatically preposterous. At the same time, it neatly epitomises Ayckbourn's idea of the English countryside as a place full of dated concepts of male honour and hidden violence.

But, although the second play has some excellent scenes, Ayckbourn temporarily loses sight of his central concern: revenge. Instead, he becomes more interested in the opposition of good and evil. Henry, redeemed and given new purpose by his love for Imogen, clearly represents good while Karen, an increasingly dark and sinister figure who has apparently burned her parents alive in a summer-house blaze, is the embodiment of unmitigated evil. In a *Sunday Times* profile Ayckbourn remarked that, 'There used to be a Christian consensus in this country about how people should behave. Now there is none. There is no moral leadership.' Ever since *Way Upstream* his plays have increasingly reflected what he sees as a spiritual crisis and, in particular, the way the moral vacuum in British life is being filled by those who enjoy the naked use of power: characters like Vince in *Way Upstream*, Vic in *Man of the Moment* and now Karen, whose upper-crust charm conceals a diabolical destructiveness.

Root-and-branch daemonism is a difficult concept to handle, and, although Karen is a fascinating character, we never quite find out what makes her tick. Is she the victim of class, environment, upbringing? Or is Ayckbourn simply saying that certain people are born with inherently warped and destructive natures? We are never quite sure; and my feeling is that Ayckbourn is far more secure with a character like Jack McCracken in *A Small Family Business* – who stumbles into moral chaos more by accident than by design – than he is with a figure of abnormal nastiness like Karen. In all his plays Ayckbourn is superb at showing how we destroy ourselves and others through small daily acts of indifference and casual cruelty. When he creates a walking monster, a female Iago, like Karen we crave more information about the circumstances that shape her.

But although *The Revengers' Comedies* is not exactly flawless, it does say something important about the vain, empty, boomerang nature of revenge. It also, in its final symmetrical scene on Albert Bridge where Henry is forced to choose between the harsh imperatives of Karen and the instinctive warmth of Imogen, shows life triumphing over death, love over hate and the continuity of existence over neurotic frenzy. It is, in the end, one of Ayckbourn's most optimistic works. It also shows him at 50 still experimenting, still pushing the frontiers outwards, still seeking that mysterious, elusive property: the perfect play. The public has always appreciated him. The signs are that critics and fellow-artists (who recently elected him, in an *Observer* poll, the Playwrights' Playwright) are beginning to realise that he is the best comic dramatist since Molière.

Chronology of Plays

(With date of first performance and publication.)

The Square Cat by 'Roland Allen'
First performed: Library Theatre, Scarborough, July 1959.
Unpublished.

Love After All by 'Roland Allen'
First performed: Library Theatre, Scarborough, December 1959.
Unpublished.

Dad's Tale by 'Roland Allen'
First performed: Library Theatre, Scarborough, December 1960.
Unpublished.

Standing Room Only by 'Roland Allen'
First performed: Library Theatre, Scarborough, July 1961.
Unpublished.

Xmas v Mastermind
First performed: Victoria Theatre, Stoke-on-Trent, December 1962.
Unpublished.

Chronology of Plays

Mr Whatnot
First performed: Victoria Theatre, Stoke-on-Trent, November 1963.
Unpublished.

Relatively Speaking
First performed (as *Meet My Father*): Library Theatre, Scarborough, July 1965.
Published: London, Evans Plays, 1968.

The Sparrow
First performed: Library Theatre, Scarborough, July 1967.
Unpublished.

How The Other Half Loves
First performed: Library Theatre, Scarborough, July 1969.
Published: London, Evans Plays, 1972.

Ernie's Incredible Illucinations
Published: London, Samuel French, 1969; Hutchinson, 1969 (in *Playbill One*, edited by Alan Durband).

Countdown
First performed: Hampstead Theatre Club, February 1969 (as part of *Mixed Doubles*).
Published: London, Methuen, 1970; Samuel French, 1977 as part of *Mixed Doubles*.

Family Circles
First performed: Library Theatre, Scarborough, August 1970 as *The Story So Far*.
Unpublished.

Time and Time Again
First performed: Library Theatre, Scarborough, July 1971.
Published: London, Samuel French, 1973.

Absurd Person Singular
First performed: Library Theatre, Scarborough, July 1972.
Published: London, Chatto and Windus, 1977 (in *Three Plays*); Penguin, 1979 (in *Three Plays*); Samuel French.

Alan Ayckbourn

The Norman Conquests
First performed: Library Theatre, Scarborough, June 1973.
Published: London, Chatto and Windus, 1975; Penguin, 1977;
Samuel French.

Absent Friends
First performed: Library Theatre, Scarborough, June 1974.
Published: London, Chatto and Windus, 1977 (in *Three Plays*);
Penguin, 1979 (in *Three Plays*); Samuel French.

Service Not Included
First transmitted: BBC 2, 1974.
Unpublished.

Confusions
First performed: Library Theatre, Scarborough, September
1974.
Published: London, Samuel French, 1977.

Jeeves
First performed: Her Majesty's, London, April 1975.
Unpublished. Original cast recording issued by MCA (MCF
2726).

Bedroom Farce
First performed: Library Theatre, Scarborough, June 1975.
Published: London, Chatto and Windus, 1977 (in *Three Plays*);
Penguin, 1979 (in *Three Plays*); Samuel French.

Just Between Ourselves
First performed: Library Theatre, Scarborough, January 1976.
Published: London, Chatto and Windus, 1979 (in *Joking Apart
and Other Plays*); Samuel French.

Ten Times Table
First performed: Stephen Joseph Theatre-in-the-Round,
Scarborough, January 1977.
Published: London, Chatto and Windus, 1979 (in *Joking Apart
and Other Plays*); Samuel French.

Chronology of Plays

Joking Apart
First performed: Stephen Joseph Theatre-in-the-Round, Scarborough, January 1978.
Published: London, Chatto and Windus, 1979 (in *Joking Apart and Other Plays*); Samuel French.

Men on Women on Men
First performed: Stephen Joseph Theatre-in-the-Round, Scarborough, June 1978. Unpublished.

Sisterly Feelings
First performed: Stephen Joseph Theatre-in-the-Round, Scarborough, January 1979.
Published: London, Chatto and Windus, 1981 (in *Sisterly Feelings and Taking Steps*).

Taking Steps
First performed: Stephen Joseph Theatre-in-the-Round, Scarborough, September 1979.
Published: London, Chatto and Windus, 1981 (in *Sisterly Feelings and Taking Steps*).

Suburban Strains
First performed: Stephen Joseph Theatre-in-the-Round, Scarborough, January 1980.
Unpublished.

First Course and Second Helping
First performed: Stephen Joseph Theatre-in-the-Round, Scarborough, July/August 1980.
Unpublished.

Season's Greetings
First performed: Stephen Joseph Theatre-in-the-Round, Scarborough, September 1980.
Published: London, Samuel French, 1982.

Me, Myself and I
First performed: Stephen Joseph Theatre-in-the-Round, Scarborough, July 1981.
Unpublished.

Alan Ayckbourn

Way Upstream
First performed: Stephen Joseph Theatre-in-the-Round, Scarborough, August 1981.
Published: London, Samuel French, 1982.

Making Tracks
First performed: Stephen Joseph Theatre-in-the-Round. Scarborough, March 1982.
Unpublished as yet.

Intimate Exchanges
First performed: Stephen Joseph Theatre-in-the-Round, Scarborough, June 1982.
Published: London, Samuel French, 1985.

A Trip to Scarborough
First performed: Stephen Joseph Theatre-in-the-Round, Scarborough, December 1982.
Unpublished as yet.

Incidental Music
First performed: Stephen Joseph Theatre-in-the-Round, Scarborough, January 1983.
Unpublished as yet.

It Could Be Any One Of Us
First performed: Stephen Joseph Theatre-in-the-Round, Scarborough, October 1983.
Unpublished.

The Seven Deadly Virtues
First performed: Stephen Joseph Theatre-in-the-Round, Scarborough, January 1984.
Unpublished.

A Chorus of Disapproval
First performed: Stephen Joseph Theatre-in-the-Round, Scarborough, May 1984.
Published: London, Faber and Faber, 1986.

Chronology of Plays

The Westwoods
First performed: Stephen Joseph Theatre-in-the-Round, Scarborough, June 1984.
Unpublished.

Woman in Mind
First performed: Stephen Joseph Theatre-in-the-Round, Scarborough, May 1985.
Published: London, Faber and Faber, 1986.

Boy Meets Girl/Girl Meets Boy
First performed: Stephen Joseph Theatre-in-the-Round, Scarborough, June 1985.
Unpublished.

Mere Soup Songs
First performed: Stephen Joseph Theatre-in-the-Round, Scarborough, June 1986.
Unpublished.

A Small Family Business
First performed: Olivier Theatre, London, June 1987.
Published: London, Faber and Faber, 1987.

Henceforward
First performed: Stephen Joseph Theatre-in-the-Round, Scarborough, July 1987.
Published: London, Faber and Faber, 1987.

Man of the Moment
First performed: Stephen Joseph Theatre-in-the-Round, Scarborough, August 1988.
Unpublished.

Mr A's Amazing Maze Plays
First performed: Stephen Joseph Theatre-in-the-Round, Scarborough, November 1988.
Unpublished.

Alan Ayckbourn

The Revengers' Comedies
First performed; Stephen Joseph Theatre-in-the-Round, Scarborough, June 1989.
Unpublished.

The Inside Outside Slide Show
First performed: Stephen Joseph Theatre-in-the-Round, Scarborough, July 1989.

Select Bibliography

Eric Bentley, *The Modern Theatre* (Robert Hale, 1948).

Eric Bentley, *The Life of the Drama* (Methuen, 1965).

John Elsom, *Post-War British Theatre* (Routledge and Kegan Paul, 1976).

Ronald Hayman, *British Theatre Since 1955* (Oxford University Press, 1979).

Stephen Joseph, *Theatre in the Round* (Barrie and Rockliff, 1967).

Oleg Kerensky, *The New British Drama* (Hamish Hamilton, 1977).

Benedict Nightingale, *An Introduction to 50 Modern British Plays* (Pan Books, 1982).

J. B. Priestley, *The Art of the Dramatist* (Heinemann, 1957).

John Russell Taylor, *The Second Wave* (Methuen, 1971).

Kenneth Tynan, *Curtains* (Longmans, 1961).

Ian Watson, *Conversations with Ayckbourn* (Macdonald, 1981).

Index

Index

Index

Index